Ice Climbing
Utah

by David S. Black

CHOCKSTONE®

FALCON®

HELENA, MONTANA

A FALCON GUIDE®

Falcon® Publishing is continually expanding its list of recreational guidebooks. All books include detailed descriptions, accurate maps, and all information necessary for enjoyable trips. You can order extra copies of this book and get information and prices for other Falcon® books by writing Falcon, P.O. Box 1718, Helena, MT 59624, or by calling toll-free 1-800-582-2665. Also, please ask for a copy of our current catalog. Visit our website at www.Falcon.com or contact us by e-mail at falcon@falcon.com.

1 2 3 4 5 6 7 8 9 10 TP 05 04 03 02 01 00

Falcon and FalconGuide are registered trademarks of Falcon® Publishing, Inc.

Front cover: Doug Heinrich on *The Candlestick,* Santaquin Canyon. Photo by John Barstow.
Back cover: Doug Heinrich on *Angel of Fear.* Photo by Chris Harmston.

Cataloging-in-Publication Data is on file at the Library of Congress.

CAUTION
Outdoor recreational activities are by their very nature potentially hazardous. All participants in such activities must assume responsibility for their own actions and safety. The information contained in this guidebook cannot replace sound judgment and good decision-making skills, which help reduce exposure, nor does the scope of this book allow for the disclosure of all the potential hazards and risks involved in such activities.

Learn as much as possible about the outdoor recreational activities in which you participate, prepare for the unexpected, and be cautious. The reward will be a safer and more enjoyable experience.

 Text pages printed on recycled paper.

TABLE OF CONTENTS

ACKNOWLEDGMENTS

When I started this project I had no idea how much work would be involved and how difficult it would be to write about climbs that melt. Researching and trying to photograph Utah's ice during the worst of three consecutively bad ice years was not easy. I would have given up on the project if it weren't for four individuals whose knowledge and encouragement made the difference: Doug Coats, Doug Heinrich, Brian Cabe, and Jason Stevens.

I have an enormous appreciation of Greg Lowe for two reasons. I would like to thank him first for the excellent article he wrote specifically for this book. Second, and more important for me, I owe him a 30-year-old debt of gratitude for pointing me toward the ice.

I would like to thank Chris Harmston and Brian Smoot for their excellent slides and information, and Jim Wright, outdoor editor for the *Ogden Standard Examiner*, for placing resources at my disposal and answering my endless questions. Thanks also to Mike Jenkins, Doug Hansen, Pat Palmieri, and Don Roberts. My appreciation also goes to John Burbidge at Falcon for his patience and encouragement.

There were probably more than a hundred people who helped with this book in one form or another. Their help was greatly appreciated.

I would like to acknowledge and thank my wife, Kristen, and our children, Kody, Darby, and Tori. For 15 years they've put up with my soloing, long periods of absence, and piles of wet gear on the living room floor. On top of it all they've somehow survived my new role as writer-ogre. Very brave souls indeed. This book is dedicated to them.

MAP LEGEND

Interstate Highway	
Paved Road (major)	
Gravel Road	
Dirt Road	
Trail	
Railroad	
Gate	
Canyon/Intermittent creek	
River/Creek	
Lake	
Camping	
Building	
Parking	Ⓟ

Interstate Highway	15
U.S. Highway	6 191
State/County Roads	23 166
City/Town	O Orem O Mona
Urban Area	
Bridge	
Peak/Elevation	x
Cliff	
Climb Number	28
Tree	
Compass	N
Scale	0 1 2 Miles

UTAH'S ICE CLIMBING AREAS

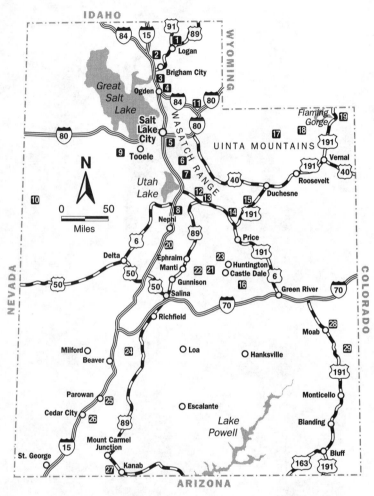

1	Logan Canyon/Bear River Range	**11**	Echo Canyon	**21**	Straight Canyon & Joes Valley
2	Wellsville Mountains	**12**	Diamond Fork Canyon	**22**	Slide and Marys Lake
3	Willard Peak	**13**	Spanish Fork Canyon	**23**	Huntington Canyon
4	Lewis Peak & Mount Ogden	**14**	Price Canyon	**24**	Tushar Mountains
5	Big & Little Cottonwood Canyons	**15**	Indian Canyon	**25**	Parowan Canyon
6	Mount Timpanogos	**16**	San Rafael Swell/Buckhorn Wash	**26**	Cedar Canyon
7	Provo Canyon	**17**	Mount Emmons	**27**	Kanab & Moqui Cave
8	Santaquin Canyon	**18**	Mount Leidy	**28**	Moab
9	Stansbury Mountains	**19**	Flaming Gorge	**29**	La Sal Mountains
10	Deep Creek Range	**20**	Maple Canyon		

Seth Shaw and Doug Heinrich on the White Angel of Fear. CHRIS HARMSTON PHOTO

INTRODUCTION

Utah is truly an incredible state. From red rock slots and blue ice to deep powder snow and rolling white water, this is one of the most diverse and spectacularly scenic areas in northern America. The recreational possibilities are easily as impressive as the scenery. Probably the best text on the state is Weir and McRae's *Utah Handbook* (Moon Publishing), recommended reading for visitors and natives alike. DeLorme's *Utah Atlas & Gazetteer* will also be very helpful. Both are available in most bookstores throughout the state.

Ice Climbing Utah describes over 200 ice climbs—the tip of a very large iceberg. Utah ice and ice climbers have played prominent roles in the evolution of American ice climbing. The developments in modern ice tool technology 30 years ago were largely a product of Utah ice climbers. To this day there is an impressive cluster of leading-edge ice climbers and innovators concentrated along the Wasatch Front.

ICE CLIMBING HISTORY

During the first half of the last century a small cadre of mountaineers and backcountry skiers was active in the Wasatch Mountains. While these pioneer alpinists thoroughly climbed and skied the mountains of northern Utah, it wasn't until the mid-1960s that ice climbs of any significance were completed. Rick Reese and Ted Wilson's step-cutting ascent of the Great White Icicle signaled the start of Utah's first modern era of ice exploration and innovation. Five to ten years later, Greg Lowe's ascent of *Malan's Waterfall* above Ogden and the completion of routes in Provo Canyon generated an enormous confidence in new ice tool technologies and helped accelerate a growing local interest in ice climbing. By the early 1980s local climbers were exploring ice routes outside the Wasatch Front. Most recently developments in mixed technologies and the completion of difficult mixed routes in Santaquin, Provo, and Maple Canyons have helped make mixed climbing—the ice climbing equivalent of sport climbing—the fastest growing variation of the sport.

It is not the purpose of this book to serve as a climbing history. Area histories are described in general, and first ascents are mentioned only when they are historically significant and there are no disputes about the climbing parties and dates.

GEOGRAPHY AND CULTURE

Utah can be divided into three physiographic provinces. The Middle Rocky Mountain Province includes the Wasatch and Bear River Ranges and the Uinta Mountains.

Greg Lowe on Malan's Waterfall, *1971.* LANCE WILCOX PHOTO—GREG LOWE COLLECTION

The impressively alpine Wasatch Mountains are 200 miles in length, running north-south from the Idaho border to central Utah. The Wasatch contain well over half of the climbs described here, and the majority of the state's commercial ski areas lie in the Wasatch just east of Salt Lake City and Ogden. The Uinta Mountains east of the Wasatch are an east-west range 150 miles in length, with two dozen peaks over 13,000 feet.

The Basin and Range Province is commonly referred to as the Great Basin. It includes the Great Salt Lake (a remnant of Lake Bonneville, an enormous Pleistocene lake) and a series of fault-block mountain ranges, including the Stansbury and Deep Creek Mountains and the House Range.

Utah's red rock country, its magnificent slot canyons, and most of the state's national parks are located in the Colorado Plateau Province. Although for most climbers the focus in this part of the state is on the desert towers and cracks, it's also home to a handful of high igneous mountain ranges. Few of the routes described in this book are located in the Colorado Plateau, but it's the author's belief that in the future many of the state's best routes will be found there.

In a nutshell, Utah's present culture is predominantly religion-based. More than two-thirds of the population is Mormon. The influence is unmistakable. Almost 90 percent of the population lives in a tight urban corridor along the west slope of the Wasatch Range. In other areas of the country this would ensure more of a diversity than it does in Utah. The majority of Utahns are still very conservative by reason of the local religious influence. Outsiders may mistake this conservatism as a cold shoulder when in reality the locals are simply occupied with trying to preserve what's left of a very controlled and comfortable environment. A case in point is the odd liquor laws. Many Utahns are shy of the influence of outsiders, including the government. Almost two-thirds of the state is controlled by the federal government (the Bureau of Land Management, the National Park Service, and the Forest Service). Because of it there are frequent clashes between the government, environmentalist "tree huggers," and multigenerational natives. This is mentioned here because climbers are invariably lumped into the "tree hugger" category. Climbers should keep that in mind when approaching landowners about access to climbing areas. With one strike already against them, it would be foolish to make matters worse by trespassing, littering, making noise, or by showing blatant disrespect for local religious beliefs. Maintaining access in Utah's rural areas is a matter of mutual trust and respect.

WINTER WEATHER: THE GOOD, THE BAD, AND THE UGLY

Utah's winter weather can range from perfect to perplexing and downright annoying. Utah is commonly thought of as a desert state, and that perception is not inaccurate for the Colorado Plateau, the Uintah Basin, and the Great Basin. The story is completely different for the mountains of northern Utah. The Wasatch and Uinta mountains receive abundant precipitation, most of it as snow.

Robbie Colbert on Contrivance, M8+, *in Provo Canyon.* CHRIS HARMSTON PHOTO

The typical winter weather pattern is one of alternating storms from the Pacific and periods of high pressure. High pressure systems create an extremely unpleasant but common phenomenon: the dreaded inversion. During an inversion, cold air becomes trapped in the valleys, and with it is trapped all the moisture and air pollutants. Above the resulting blanket of dense fog and smog the sun is bright and temperatures are warm. The worst inversions can last weeks, freezing insignificant low-altitude valley seeps into climbing shape and virtually destroying the major climbs in the canyons. While the skiers bask in warm, sunny skies and gorgeous sunsets on the slopes, downtown it's a murky, depressing, and unhealthy environment that will only clear out when another cold front blows through.

Most of Utah's precipitation falls in the form of snow. The high altitudes and low humidity ensure an abundance of powder snow. The state brags of the "greatest snow on earth," and it's probably no exaggeration. However, the same conditions that make Utah a magical place to ski also make it a dangerous place for backcountry travelers. Avalanches have taken numerous lives, and the number of deaths per year is on the rise. There are probably very few active backcountry skiers and winter climbers who have not been caught in or at least witnessed potentially disastrous slides. This hazard cannot be taken lightly. Newcomers to this sport are advised to read and re-read the accompanying article by Mike Jenkins and Liz Hebertson of the Bear River Avalanche Information Center and to consult additional manuals on the subject. Anybody who is serious about winter backcountry travel should also take an avalanche class that includes field study.

CLIMBING HAZARDS AND SAFETY

Ice climbing is inherently dangerous, probably more so than rock climbing in general. It's beyond the scope of this text to present a wordy lecture on climbing safety, but a few simple words of caution are warranted:

- Ice varies from year to year, and the perception of difficulty and commitment varies from climber to climber. Do not assume the descriptions and ratings in this book are accurate.

- Wear a helmet and eye protection on every climb. Some Utah routes are notoriously crowded, and if a half-dozen or so parties are banging away at the ice above you, falling ice can become an extreme hazard.

- Avoid soloing.

- As much as reasonably possible remain roped and belayed while traversing above cliff hazards.

- Become knowledgeable about avalanches. Always get a forecast before the climb. Take reliable avalanche gear with you, and be sure to turn your transceiver on.

Bruce Bidner on the remains of Angel of Fear. BRIAN CABE PHOTO

- Back up fixed gear when possible. There are many old, unreliable bolts and fixed pitons.

- Always yell, "Ice!" or "Rock!" to warn those below if you dislodge ice or rocks or see/hear falling debris. If you hear such a warning, lean into the slope or duck under a protective feature, and avoid looking up.

- Keep an eye on the weather. Get a forecast beforehand.

- Carry clothing for a colder and wetter climb than you expect.

SNOW AVALANCHES AND ICE CLIMBING IN UTAH'S MOUNTAINS

by Mike Jenkins and Liz Hebertson

Snow avalanches are a common feature of the Utah mountain landscape. The combination of heavy annual snowfall, wind, and steep slopes results in potential instabilities in the layered mountain snowpack.

The Utah mountains receive 22 to 25 inches of precipitation annually, most of it falling in the winter as snow. This amounts to 200 to 600 inches of annual snow at elevations above 7,000 feet. It is not unusual to receive 1 to 4 feet of snow in a single storm cycle. The most significant weather factor contributing to the formation and release of avalanches is wind. Wind speed and direction varies with elevation, latitude, and topography. Average wind speeds at 8,000 feet are 15 to 20 miles per hour with speeds increasing at higher elevations. In general, winds greater than 15 miles per hour transport snow from windward aspects and deposit it as wind slabs on lee slopes.

Of the elements contributing to avalanche potential, terrain is the most constant. Most slab avalanches occur on slopes with steepnesses between 30 and 45 degrees. Aspect, or the direction a slope faces, affects wind loading and exposure to sun. Midwinter avalanches are most common on north, northeast, and east facing slopes. Colder temperatures cause the development of weaker snow, and slopes with these aspects are most often loaded by prevailing winds. Other terrain features that influence avalanche occurrence are elevation, slope configuration (e.g., convex vs. concave), and the presence of gullies, cirques, and vegetation.

There are several types of avalanches, including loose snow, cornice falls, ice and slab avalanches. The most dangerous are slab avalanches. The mountain snowpack is ever changing. It is subject to additional snowfall and erosion by wind and sun, which results in a characteristic "layered" pattern. Slab avalanches are possible when a cohesive layer (the slab) is separated by a weak layer from a bed surface below. When the stress on a slab exceeds the strength that holds it in place, the potential for a slab avalanche exists. Most natural slab avalanches occur during or shortly after significant loading by additional new snow, rain, or wind-redeposited snow. If natural avalanches do not occur within this period it is likely that the snowpack will eventually adjust to the new load.

Avalanche warnings at Aspen Grove. DAVE BLACK PHOTO

Most human-triggered avalanches occur before the snowpack has had sufficient time to stabilize. Encounters between humans and avalanches have increased in recent years in Utah and North America in general. One obvious reason for this is the increased numbers of people engaged in winter backcountry travel and recreation. Another is that technological advances in skis, snowboards, snowshoes, and snow machines enable users to more easily access dangerous avalanche terrain. Most avalanche accidents occur when the victim or a member of the victim's party triggers a slab avalanche.

Frozen waterfalls and sections of steep ice (i.e., ice climbs) often form in couloirs or gullies at the bases of talus slopes with large, wind loaded, avalanche starting zones above. From an avalanche terrain perspective, these are among the most dangerous of terrain traps. In addition, ice climbers approach avalanche paths from below and can be exposed to the avalanche dangers for prolonged periods of time when routes are long or difficult. Weather conditions can also change during the time it takes to complete long routes. Warming of the starting zone above, additional snowfall or wind loading can increase the avalanche danger during the course of a climb. The smallest of ice or snow avalanches can knock solo or free ice climbers off the route. Trauma is often the cause of death, even if climbers are wearing helmets. Climbers are often roped together and create the potential for multiple victims even if only one climber is knocked off the route by an avalanche.

Avalanche awareness, route selection, stability evaluation, and hazard assessment are essential in preventing backcountry avalanche incidents. The most obvious sign of instability is recent avalanching. Other clues to instability include collapsing or hollow sounds, shooting cracks, and evidence of recent wind loading. A variety of snowpack stability tests can be conducted to look for slabs, weak layers, and bed surfaces. These tests include shear and compression tests often performed in snow pits dug in safe locations similar to slopes in question. The nature of ice climbing makes stability evaluation difficult since conditions in the starting zone are often hard to assess. Ice climbing is best avoided when avalanche conditions are present and natural avalanches are likely. Assessment should be conducted prior to the climb by contacting the local avalanche forecast center.

In Utah the forecast center numbers are:

Provo area (385) 378-4333

Salt Lake City area (801) 364-1581

Alta (801) 742-0830

Park City (435) 658-5512

Ogden (385) 626-8700

Logan (435) 797-4146

Moab (435) 259-7669

Or visit www.avalanche.org

Having the necessary search and rescue equipment and possessing the ability to execute an avalanche rescue are essential for ice climbers under any conditions. Equipment includes avalanche transceivers worn by all parties at all times, a shovel, and probe. If caught in an avalanche, try to stay near the surface and create an air space around your face. If your partner has been caught, identify the point last seen. Buried victims are often located at the toe of the avalanche debris below the point last seen. After assessing further danger, look for visible signs of the victim on the surface of the debris. Equipment and articles of clothing can also provide clues to the victim's location. Use your beacon and probe to locate the victim. Once located, leave your probe in place and dig down to the victim. The chances of survival decrease very rapidly with time elapsed, reaching about 50 percent after 30 minutes. Practice in the quick and efficient use of rescue equipment is very important and should be done regularly during the climbing season.

Avalanche education is important to gain the knowledge necessary for safe travel, climbing, and rescue in avalanche terrain. Numerous sources of avalanche information are available from avalanche forecast centers, universities, and other organizations.

Editor's Note: Mike Jenkins and Liz Hebertson can be contacted at the Bear River Avalanche Information Center, Utah State University, Logan, Utah 84322-5215.

ACCESS AND ETHICS

Again, this is not the place for a lengthy lecture on ethics. Some basic principles are emphasized:

- Pick up your trash.

- Use the toilet at home. Don't urinate or defecate on or near trails or at the base of a climb where everyone has to sit to put on their crampons and set up their belays.

- Don't drive your two-wheel drive vehicle up a narrow, snowy road. If you get stuck, so will everyone who follows and you'll block the road until the mess can be resolved.

- Don't park on the road. Find a pullout, even if you have to dig one out by shovel.

- Don't even consider disturbing archaeological sites. Several of the climbs described in this book are located adjacent to dwelling sites and rock art. Don't touch them.

- Don't put bolts where there are logical clean alternatives.

- Respect posted property. Get permission to cross private lands when possible.

- Occasionally in this book I make reference to "farmed" routes. These are manmade ice routes created by purposefully dripping water down a rock face until it freezes into an ice climb. Some climbers consider this practice to be unethical. It is not my intention to take a stance one way or another on the ethics of farming routes, but where the practice takes place, it is mentioned in the route description.

Using this Guide

Each section of route descriptions is prefaced by an area summary which includes a brief introduction, a short and very generic climbing history, information on how to get to the area, a general description of the climbing environment, tips on the climbing season, an explanation of ethics and access issues for the area, a list of USGS maps, a list of guidebooks and guide services, information on where to camp or sleep, where to find basic services, what to do in emergencies, and where to go for additional climbing or skiing.

Routes are described by name, overall excellence (0-3 stars), technical grade, commitment rating, length, approach, route characteristics (climb), and descent. MM represents mile marker.

At the end of the book are appendices listing suggested further reading and important phone numbers and addresses. Finally, an alphabetical index lists all proper nouns, including routes and proper names.

THE RATING SYSTEM

Even at the time of this writing—several generations after the controversy first started to brew—there still does not seem to be a universally accepted rating system for ice climbs and mixed climbs in the United States. Even when two experienced climbers from the same part of the country describe the same climb under the same conditions, using the same rating system, chances are their ratings will differ. Not only do personalities make ice ratings difficult, but the fact that ice conditions vary so extensively from one week to another (and even worse from one year to another) makes ratings highly unreliable. In addition, rating criteria vary significantly from book to book. The routes described in this book are rated by technical grade and by commitment. Seriousness ratings are not indicated in this book (see explanation below).

Technical grade: Technical grade is largely determined by the angle and sustained nature of the climbing, the thickness and features of the ice, the ease of placing good protection, and the adequacy of belays. Technical grades for this text are based on the single hardest pitch on a route and are summarized as follows, in order from grade 1 to grade 7:

1: Hiking with crampons; barely ascending at angles up to 30 degrees.

2: Fairly easily climbed with one tool at angles of 30 to 60 degrees; ice that is commonly thick and solid; a few very short steps at steeper angles.

3: Sustained climbing at angles of 60 to 80 degrees; two tools are normally used but the weight is on the feet; protection is generally good; belays and resting places are adequate.

Last Chance Falls.
BRETT FULLER PHOTO

4: Continuous climbing at 75 to 85 degrees, or a less steep pitch with significant vertical; generally good ice; sustained but interrupted by good belays; acceptable protection.

5: Sustained 85- to 90-degree ice; most of the pitch is vertical; protection hard to place but may be adequate.

6: Full pitch of vertical; usually free standing (barely or not touching); less than good ice; resting places scarce; hanging belays; very questionable protection.

7: Continuously vertical or overhanging; thin ice of a poor quality and doubtful adhesion; generally unprotectable.

These grades are assigned to each route under its most common conditions or under the conditions in which it is most frequently climbed. In some systems these grades are given in Roman numerals. Current grades can vary radically with local weather and seasonal conditions.

Technical grades are prefixed with letters that indicate the type of ice. Water ice (WI) is essentially seasonal or permanent ice that has formed through the freezing of meltwater or rain. It can range from brittle to slushy. Alpine ice (AI) is permanent ice that has formed as a result of consolidation and metamorphosis of snow. It can range from cork-like hard snow to cement-like "black ice." Mixed (M) routes include both ice and rock climbing.

Mixed technical grades (M1 through M10) are very difficult to equate precisely to rock climbing classifications or technical ice grades. Dry-tooling (climbing rock using ice tools) is neither traditional rock climbing nor traditional ice climbing, and cannot be equated to traditional grades and ratings. However, if we were to attempt such an equation, it could be said that M5 is very roughly reminiscent of 5.9 rock climbing, M6 of 5.10, M7 of 5.11, M8 of 5.12, M9 of 5.13, etc.

Seriousness ratings: Seriousness ratings (PG, R, X) are not used in this guide. However, it can be assumed that any climb rated WI6 or harder is a very difficult and hazardous undertaking. It can also be assumed that virtually any ice climb has the potential to be extremely serious and difficult if conditions are less than ideal, and sometimes even when they are ideal.

Commitment ratings: A commitment rating is indicated with each route. These ratings are based on the length of the approach and descent, the remoteness of the climb, the length of the climb, the nature of the climbing, and the type and sustained nature of objective hazards. In this text commitment ratings are determined as follows:

I: The climb is short and near the road, trailhead, or basecamp; easy descent; no objective hazard; easy, solid belays.

II: The climb is a short distance from the road or trailhead; the approach requires some winter travel skills; relatively easy rappel or downclimb descent; climbing may take several hours; little or occasional objective hazard.

III: The climb may require an approach of a few hours or is a multipitch route closer to the road, trailhead, or basecamp; descent requires rappels or exposed downclimbing; climbing takes most of a day; possible avalanche hazard.

IV: A long approach requiring mountaineering skills; descent may be difficult or very technical; the climb may take a long day; definite objective hazards with a possible hazardous descent.

V: A climb in a remote setting in a technical canyon or high on a mountain; descent requires multiple rappels; a long multipitch climb taking at least one day; sustained avalanche, rockfall, or crevasse hazard.

VI: A difficult and lengthy approach into a very remote alpine or technical canyon setting with possible logistical problems (multiple camps; caching; ferrying loads; fixed lines, etc.); complicated descent; a multiday climb with sustained difficulty; constant objective hazard.

VII: Similar to VI but requiring several days for the approach; sustained exposure to major objective hazards.

Star ratings: Rating of one★, two★★, or three★★★ stars are occasionally used to indicate routes of exceptional quality.

THE TOOL CONNECTION

by Greg Lowe

Ice climbing has always been a marriage of tools and technique. Beginning with glacier walks and alpenstocks, steeper terrain dictated the invention of crampons, ice axes, and the use of ropes, carabiners, and anchors. By the mid-1930s, basic crampon design had been improved by adding front points (an improvement generated by Larent Grivel), and Willo Welzenbach and partners had drooped their ice axe picks to the proper angle necessary for climbing steep ice without cutting steps.

The bold ice routes pioneered by Welzenbach utilized the newest technology to expand the ice climbing experience. It would be many years before Welzenbach's routes would be eclipsed due to improved climbing techniques and tools.

During World War II, the initial momentum created by Welzenbach and others almost came to a halt. Nearly every able-bodied person was recruited for service and nationalistic interests prevailed. A dark cloud hung over mountaineering and the world itself. Ice and snow climbing techniques were seen as primarily useful in moving troops over difficult glaciers and alpine passes. Rock climbing techniques were to be utilized by assault teams, and the idea of "conquering" a mountain had devolved from the concept of conquering an enemy. Such mindset was a by-product of the struggles of the period. It was difficult enough to stay alive—why chance death needlessly?

Although these dark clouds were raining heavily on the art of mountaineering during this time, a glimmer of sunshine soon emerged. By the early 1950s, a new generation of climbers began to rediscover the joys of mountaineering. In all but a few locations, the concept of steep, stepless ice climbing had been nearly forgotten. The newer techniques developed by the French began to reverse this trend and were very effective for covering large expanses of ice and snow, but were not focused on near-vertical and overhanging ice. As a by-product of their long mountaineering tradition, the Scots began to pioneer difficult ice on Ben Nevis. However, it was an American, Yvon Chouinard, who rediscovered and refined the drooped-pick ice axe necessary to emulate and expand upon the techniques pioneered by Welzenbach.

During this development period, the Scots, led by Hamish MacInnes, developed the extreme droop known as the "Terrordactyl," and were successful in ascending many of the obvious ice routes on Ben Nevis. The bold leads performed by the best climbers of the 1950s and 1960s lacked only two things: extended verticality and solid protection. With the refinement of the ice screw, both were about to be addressed.

By the late 1960s, American ice climbing had fallen far behind the European community. Ice was seen primarily as an obstacle to get over or around. With the exception of the northwest, little true ice potential existed in the continental United States other than alpine gullies in summer (such as the Black Ice Couloir) or frozen waterfalls in winter. Prior to the introduction of the Chouinard/Frost tools, the most difficult climbs were steep, step-cutting events.

The Lowe party on the first winter ascent of the Black Ice Couloir, *1971.*
GREG LOWE COLLECTION

It was essentially at the end of the 1960s that modern American steep-ice climbing began. Gullies that had been traditionally climbed by cutting steps were now repeated by climbers using only the front points and ice axe as an anchor. This technique could logically be extended up to and beyond vertical ice, meaning that the common winter waterfall was now a possibility. But further evolution of tools and techniques would be required, since ice steeper than 80 degrees necessitates near-total reliance on the hooking and staying power of the hand tools. Also, the rudimentary ice screws of the time were particularly difficult to place while on such steep ice. What was needed was a good development ground.

After completing the first winter ascent of the Black Ice Couloir on the Grand Teton in January 1971 with my brother Jeff and cousins George and Dave Lowe, I (who had done none of the leading on the climb) felt that it would be beneficial to study ice craft on steeper ice conditions. Having been introduced to curved tool techniques by Yvon Chouinard on the Teton Glacier in the summer of 1970, I knew that further adaptation of tools and techniques might be necessary before delicate waterfall routes could be accomplished safely and efficiently. This medium was substantially different from gully or glacial ice. It became my quest to explore these differences. Luckily, within walking distance of my backyard was a perfect training ground. Located on the southwest side of Malan's Peak was a beautiful, 300-foot-high waterfall. I focused my efforts there.

Every day for several weeks I hiked up the moderate approach to the falls to test equipment and techniques. Though occasionally accompanied by Scott Etherington, Lance Wilcox and others, I spent most of the time bouldering and testing equipment by myself. As my awkward, initial forays became smoother and more refined, I began to feel comfortable on vertical ice. Lance began the task of helping me modify screws and recurve and retooth Chouinard and InterAlp axes and hammers for the specialized techniques required. After determining that the modifications were effective, I decided to test them on a multipitch climb.

On an early morning in March of 1971, my partner Rob Brown and I approached the base of Malan's Waterfall in a light snowstorm. This represented ideal conditions, since the climb faces southwest and is a dangerous place during sunny days. After sorting equipment, I began the first lead. Since we had only one set of modified tools, and I was more comfortable on ice, Rob agreed to belay and follow on jumars. The first couple of leads were straightforward, steep ice with occasional vertical sections. Since we had only six Salewa screws and five Marwa "coat hangers," the main problem was placing protection. The Salewas tended toward constipation while the Marwas fractured the ice out. Because of this, the leads were kept relatively short.

The third pitch represented the crux, since it had formed a gently overhanging mushroom at the top of the falls. With much trepidation, I stemmed and hooked my way up beneath the bulge. Since I had saved much of my rack for use under and through the bulge, it was with consternation that I realized at the base of the final bulge that the friable quality of the ice—and the difficulty I was having hanging by my tools and placing protection—prevented me from setting reliable anchors. I placed a Marwa coat hanger just below the final bulge and set out to surmount it.

After considerable cleaning (i.e., thrashing) of icicles, I planted both axes on the bulge and stemmed and knee-locked under the mushroom cap. After much contortion, I was able to place the right tool, a Chouinard axe, above the bulge and mantle onto my left tool while cranking on the right. Squatting high on my front points, I removed the left tool and replanted it. Two placements later I was on easy ground, though running water and a precarious gap between the ice and rock hastened my placement of a knifeblade in the quartzite at the top. After struggling with some slipping jumars, Rob joined me and we finished up the short gully ramp above the falls. An hour later, we were loading my Subaru in the twilight, tired but satisfied.

The ice axe modifications had worked well, but the anchors were nearly worthless. With this in mind, we began developing tubular drive-in, screw-out anchors. These we named Snargs. Since Rob had access to a machine shop and welder, the first Snargs were machined and assembled by Rob. Other waterfall climbs soon followed; our Snargs and the newer Chouinard screws quickly became the anchors of choice. By 1974, American ice climbing was at the forefront of the rest of the world, and with Jeff Lowe and Mike Weiss's climb of Bridalveil Falls in Colorado, pure ice climbing had essentially peaked.

With additional refinement of hand tools, anchors, and replacement of the traditional Chouinard crampons with Footfangs and their derivatives, ice climbing and rock climbing are beginning to approach similar levels of maximum difficulty. Since most climbs nowadays are mixed rock and ice, and the ice generally consists of thin ice, hanging curtains, and icicles, the risk of injury is also increasing. Perhaps the continuing evolution of tools will not only enhance developing techniques but also address this increasing risk of injury. In no other area of climbing is the reward of tool evolution more apparent than in ice climbing, and for ice climbers, at least, these benefits appear to outweigh the risks.

MIXING IT UP. . .

By Doug Heinrich

My idea of mixed climbing 20 years ago was scratching my way up a couloir in the Tetons with my piolet and flexible crampons, heading for the summit. I really didn't think much of mixed climbing, at least I didn't consider it a specific genre of climbing; rather, it was what you did to gain the summit. Twenty-three years after I first summited the Grand Teton at the age of 14, I find myself dry-tooling out a cave in Santaquin Canyon, wondering if it's M9 or M9-. Things have changed, and I'm happy to be part of the evolution of mixed climbing.

At the time of this writing, I've just returned from the Canadian Rockies, most likely the best waterfall ice climbing in the world. Sean Isaac, a friend from Canmore, Alberta said, "This is the golden age of mixed climbing." He might very well be

Doug Heinrich on Swollen Cheek, M7+, *in Santaquin Canyon.* CHRIS HARMSTON PHOTO

Chris Harmston on Ricochet, M6+, *in Santaquin Canyon.* DOUG HEINRICH PHOTO

right—the Rockies have 135 new mixed lines that have "gone in" in the last two seasons. Similar trends are happening in Colorado, Europe, and Utah. It reminds me of climbing in Idaho's City of Rocks in the 1970s; we didn't even *see* the face climbs that are there today. It's funny how you can look at the same face and see or not see the possibility of the lines depending on your state of mind. I'm sure 20 years from now climbers will be discovering new endeavors we never dreamed would go.

It seems that traditional ice climbing has a difficulty cap which reaches into the easy 5.12 range. However, the new "modern" mixed lines combine the techniques of hard sport climbing and difficult ice climbing to produce a range of difficulty venturing into the 5.13+ (M10) range. My main interest in developing new "modern" mixed lines is due to the fact that we have recently experienced a series of warm winters, and many of the traditional ice lines have not formed; because of this, we have essentially figured out a new hybrid sport that allows us to climb onto hanging curtains and daggers without the use of aid. Most of the routes in Santaquin or Provo canyons are bolted due to the poor quality of the limestone, while the routes in Maple Canyon are a mixed bag of cams, nuts, pins, and bolts. These routes range from less-than-vertical to severely overhanging caves. The moves require a steady hand, power, endurance, and a keen eye to figure out the sequences first try.

The new generation of mixed climbs has opened up more lines in the traditional areas, allowing climbers to ascend the standard ice climbs a few times and then venture onto mixed lines. Often these mixed lines link up parts of regular routes with a little dry-tooling in between the sections of ice; sometimes these mixed routes take independent lines that never completely form. This has opened a new learning opportunity for most of us, and we've developed techniques for standing on rock with crampons and hooking our tools on small edges, pockets, slopers, and cracks. A broad base of rock, ice, and aid climbing skills are required to succeed on today's mixed routes.

I'm always excited about climbing when I'm learning. Mixed climbing allows us to look at the standard flows in a new light, to see sections of ice and rock and figure out ways to go there. It has opened up a new world of techniques and possibilities—so get out there and check it out and add a little spice to the regular ice.

Below I've listed some of my favorite mixed routes:

PROVO CANYON

- *Stairway to Heaven* has mixed variations on each pitch—check them out! Pitch 1: Various thin mixed lines that are easy to toprope. Pitch 2: Far left (M4)—needs a few cams; left center (M8 depending on the ice)—5 bolts to a dagger. Pitch 3: Left of main flow (M7)—4 bolts of thin mixed, then traverse right to the ice. Pitch 4: Left of main flow (M7), right of *Prophet on a Stick*—2 bolts mixed to a dagger. Pitch 5: Called *Contrivance* (M8+), left of main pillar, steep dry-tooling to hanging curtain. Pitch 6: Chimney (M5)—requires rock gear.

- *Upper Bridalveil Falls*

M7 right of farmed 200' pillar—4 bolts to curtain.

M9 (*Bruceipher*), second tier left of 200-foot pillar—5 bolts to series of drips.

SANTAQUIN CANYON

- *Swollen Cheek* (M7+, VI)—6 bolts; between *Automatic* and *Candlestick*.

- *Ricochet* (M6+, VII)—10 bolts; two pitches of mixed to the left of *Angel of Fear.*

- *Better Than Baghdad* (M8)—Cave four minutes from start of *Squash Head,* 5 bolts to pillar.

MAPLE CANYON

- *Jesus Wept* (M6, V+)—Main Box Canyon; all natural pro.

- *Sandbagger* (M4, III)—Main Box Canyon; all natural pro.

- *Empire of Dirt* (M6, VI)—Main Box Canyon; all natural pro.

- *Golden Showers* (M6, VI)—Upper Box Canyon; pins, cams, nuts.

- *Phen Fen* (M6, V)—Upper Box Canyon; 2 bolts.

- *Bottomless Topless* (M7, VI+)—main road; pins, cams, nuts.

- *Titanic* (M6, VI)—main road; 3 bolts.

- *Sir Mix a Lot* (M6, VI)—Left Hand Fork; 2 bolts.

- *Ice 800* (M8, V)—above *Frankenchrist,* left of Margarita Cave; 10 bolts.

THE BEAR RIVER RANGE

The Bear River Range closely parallels the far northern Wasatch Range and between them is Cache Valley and the city of Logan. Logan Canyon is the site of some excellent limestone rock climbing and a substantial amount of ice. The area has a reputation for being a poor destination for ice climbers, yet the truth is that even in the mildest of winters there is good ice somewhere in Logan Canyon.

Logan sits 90 miles north of Salt Lake City at the mouth of Logan Canyon on the west slope of the Bear River Range. The principal road from Salt Lake City to Jackson Hole and the Tetons (US Highway 89) goes through the city and up Logan Canyon and provides easy access to the climbs described in this chapter.

Climbing history: Most of the reliable roadside routes in the Logan area were climbed in the late 1960s and early 1970s. Data on these first ascents is conflicting and includes parties from Logan, Brigham City, Ogden, Salt Lake City, and Provo.

Getting there: From Interstate 15 north of Honeyville, take exit 388 and drive east on Utah 30 to Logan. From I-15 near Brigham City, take US 89/91 through Sardine Canyon to Logan. Continue through Logan and into Logan Canyon on US 89.

General Description: There are about two dozen established ice climbs in Logan Canyon, ranging from 20 to 160 feet. The altitude of the climbing ranges from 4,800 to 6,000 feet. These are some of the most fickle climbs in the state. Many either melt out quickly or don't form at all. The climbs generally are seeps and pipeline leaks which form over limestone or shale. Although a number of mixed routes have been done, most have not seen second ascents, and their locations are unclear. Take a few pieces of rock gear along on most Logan Canyon climbs. Always wear a helmet. Use extreme caution when crossing the river.

Climbing season: Like the climbs themselves, the overall season is hard to predict. Late December to early January is probably the best time for the roadside ice. A few of the off-road routes (e.g., *Last Chance Falls*) are likely to be in shape until early March.

Ethics and access: There is an agreement between the Forest Service and local climbers to restrict climbing on certain crags in Logan Canyon in order to protect endangered plant species. Although this generally does not have much effect on ice climbers because of the limited numbers and locations of ice routes, it would be in everyone's best interest for visiting climbers to get updated information on closures and restrictions. The Forest Service can be contacted by visiting their location on US 89 just

THE BEAR RIVER RANGE

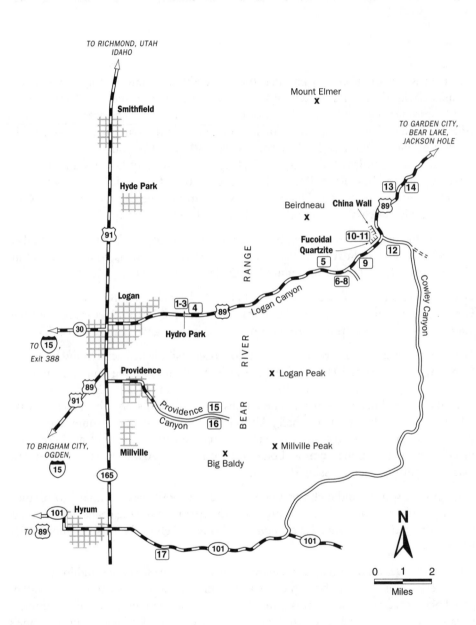

TO RICHMOND, UTAH
IDAHO

Mount Elmer
X

Smithfield

TO GARDEN CITY,
BEAR LAKE,
JACKSON HOLE

Hyde Park

13 14

Beirdneau   China Wall
X

89

91

Fucoidal
Quartzite

10-11

RANGE

5   9

Logan

1-3 4

6-8

89   Logan Canyon

12

Cowley Canyon

30

Hydro Park

TO 15,
Exit 388

RIVER

X Logan Peak

89

Providence

91

Providence   15
Canyon   16

BEAR

TO BRIGHAM CITY,
OGDEN,

15

Millville

X
Big Baldy

X Millville Peak

165

101 Hyrum

TO 89

N

17   101   101

0   1   2
Miles

before the hill leading into Logan Canyon. Also, consider checking with the local climbing shops. Tim Monsell's guidebook *Logan Canyon Climbs* contains a detailed summary of the policy in effect in the late 1990s.

There has been a modest movement afoot to limit the number of bolts in Logan Canyon. It's reasonable to expect climbers to be conservative with bolt placement.

Maps: USGS: Temple Peak; Mt. Elmer; Logan Peak; Logan; Paradise.

Other guidebooks: *Logan Canyon Climbs* by Tim Monsell.

Gear and guides: Logan has two sources of climbing gear: The Trailhead and Adventure Sports (see Appendix B). Check with these establishments regarding local guiding or instruction.

Camping and accommodations: Logan Canyon is packed with fee and non-fee campgrounds. There are plenty of hotels or motels in the city.

Services: Logan is a town of nearly 45,000 residents and a large university. All services are available.

Emergency services: Call 911 for all emergencies. Most of the area's ice routes are short and close enough to the road that technical rescue will not be an issue, and Cache County's responders can adequately handle most problems. Medical helicopters are available from the Wasatch Front. Logan has one large hospital. For avalanche conditions, call the forecast center (Appendix C).

Nearby climbing and skiing: A couple of short routes can be found at Cutler Dam (west on Utah 30). Access is an issue there. Get permission from Utah Power to both park and climb. There is excellent ice above Willard and Ogden to the south. Commercial skiing is available at Beaver Mountain, northeast of Logan on US 89. East of Ogden are Snowbasin, Powder Mountain, and Nordic Valley.

LOGAN CANYON

1. FIVE FINGERS (WI2–3, I)

Length: 150 feet.

Approach: Just beyond the entrance to the Hydro Park on the north side of the mouth of Logan Canyon (MM 374.8), look sharply left. This route lies in a choppy, east-facing gully that comes down to the road.

The Climb: Climb easy ice directly up the gully.

Descent: Walk off.

2. WEEPING WALL (WI3, I)

Length: Up to 60 feet.

Approach: From the Hydro Park entrance, this is a 5-minute walk up-canyon to a cliff directly behind the power station.

The Climb: The wall can actually produce 3 or more climbable lines and often forms a wide curtain of from 10 feet high on the left to 60 feet on the right.

Descent: Easy rappel from trees.

Note: About 20 yards to the right of the *Weeping Wall* curtain is a low-angle arete which drops down from the obvious cement structure on the pipeline. Early in the 1999–2000 season there was a nice WI2 smear (farmed) running a full pitch the length of this buttress.

3. POWER ALLEY (WI2–3, I)

Length: 40–160 feet.

Approach: From the power plant hike 100 yards up the side road to a steep gully in the cliff.

The Climb: The ice is very unpredictable. Some years there may be only 40 feet. Other years it can form all the way up to the pipeline. Often there are 2 distinct lines, one in the deep cleft on the left side of the gully and another on a dihedral ramp to the right.

Descent: Rappel from trees or hike off.

4. FRIGID WHEN WET (WI2–3, I)

Length: 30–60 feet.

Approach: Drive up the canyon to the first bridge past the first dam (MM 375.25). Park off to the right just before the bridge. Cross the river and hike north along the base of the limestone cliff. 10 minutes. It's also possible to hike up the mountainside just east of the bridge and rappel from trees to the base of the cliff.

The Climb: This usually forms in a wide gully as 3 or 4 separate steep lines of 30 to 40 feet, with the upper 10 feet or so near vertical. In the 1999–2000 season a farmed route formed on a face 30 feet to the right of *Frigid*. It consisted of a 15-foot-wide curtain, 60 feet in length.

Descent: Rappel (trees) or walk off.

Note: Between the Hydro Plant and *Skatie's Tears* are a number of seeps and very short cliffs that form obscure columns and curtains. An example is *Roadside Attraction* (MM 374.45). This text does not describe routes less than 10m (33 feet) in length.

5. SKATIE'S TEARS (WI3, I)

Length: 35 feet.

Approach: This short route is located on the left (north) side of the road near MM 380.5. It's been described by some as being in the "Fucoidal Quartzite" and this has led to some confusion. While it does in fact form in a fucoidal quartzite crag, it is NOT located at the popular Fucoidal Quartzite tourist pullout (MM 383.2).

The Climb: The route forms on the left side of an alcove in a crag and consists of a thin column with a mantle finish.

Descent: Rappel or hike off.

In the crags across the canyon from *Skatie's Tears* several thin and mixed lines have been climbed. They require a 15-minute approach and are very short (less than 50 feet, with walkoff descents) and are not described here in detail.

Note: The next 6 routes rarely come into shape.

6. CO-DEPENDENT CHICKS (WI3-4, I)

Length: 160 feet (not including a short hike between sections).

Approach: This route is located on the south side of the canyon, across from MM 381. Cross the bridge at MM 381.5 and walk a half-mile downstream.

The Climb: Climb a 40-foot curtain. Slog 25 yards to a 25-foot pillar and continue up and left on very steep ice, then up a few bulges and short steps and up a gully.

Descent: 2-rope rappel from a large tree.

7. SNOWBOARD CHICKS DIG SKIERS (WI4, M4, I)

Length: 50–80 feet.

Approach: This is located on the south side at MM 381.1. Park at MM 381.5 across a bridge at a gate, then walk 2,000 feet down the canyon.

The Climb: Ascend a 15-foot pillar and traverse right about 5 yards to another short pillar. The climb ends in an alcove with a tree.

Descent: Rappel from a tree.

8. HOW DO YOU LIKE THEM APPLES (WI2, I)

Length: 80 feet.

Approach: This is also located on the south side of the canyon across the river from MM 381.2. Cross at the bridge at MM 381.5 and walk 1,500 feet down the canyon.

The Climb: This is a 70-foot slab with short vertical steps.

Descent: Rappel.

9. SWEET SURRENDER (WI2–3, I)

Length: 60–80 feet.

Approach: At MM 382 park and cross the bridge. Hike uphill several hundred yards to the base of a yellow cliff.

The Climb: Climb slab ice, bulges, and short vertical steps.

Descent: Hike off.

10. CHINA CAT SUNFLOWER (WI4, I)

Length: 150 feet.

Approach: Park in the paved parking area at MM 383 and walk a quarter-mile up-canyon past the Fucoidal Quartzite geologic site.

The Climb: This route is a 5.5 rock climb known as *The Alcove*, located high on a smooth slab with an inverted 'Y' crack system.

Descent: Hike off.

11. DRINKING ON BORROWED TIME (WI3, I)

Length: 115 feet.

Approach: The climb is located a few feet uphill from a rock climbing route known as *Gully Washer*, in a gully near MM 383.6 just before the crag known as China Wall.

The Climb: Climb a 10-foot column and continue up over gully ice and a few short curtains.

Descent: Rappel from trees or hike off.

12. LAST CHANCE FALLS (WI3, I)

Length: 90 feet.

Approach: Take the Right-Hand Fork (Camp Lomia and Cowley Canyon) turnoff and ski, hike, or drive 0.8 mile (4WD only) to a picnic area about 500 yards past a curious green sighting pipe. The route is south of the road, across the stream and high on the slope in a notch in the cliffs.

The Climb: Ascend 65 feet of steep ice to a final 25 feet of near-vertical.

Descent: Rappel from trees (2 ropes).

13. BRIDGE ACROSS FOREVER (WI3–4, I)

Length: 80 feet.

Approach: Park at MM 385.7 (the "Rodent Ranch"). Cross the bridge and hike down-canyon for 200 yards, then uphill 20 minutes to the base of the climb.

The Climb: Steppy ice in a corner with several short curtains.

Descent: Rappel from trees.

14. SLIPPERY WHEN WET (WI2–4, I)

Length: 150–180 feet.

Approach: Park at MM 385.6 and follow a trail toward the north slope cliffs. High in the gully take a faint trail left (northwest) and follow it to the base of the climb. 20–30 minutes.

The Climb: A steppy, low-angle seep with bulges.

Descent: Rappel from trees.

PROVIDENCE CANYON

15. ANGEL'S TIERS (WI3, I)

Length: 100–150 feet.

Approach: From US 89 drive east along Utah 238 through Providence to 100 East, then follow it south as it becomes South Canyon Road and turns toward the canyon along 600 South. Park low in the canyon unless you have high-clearance 4WD. A quarry is located 3 miles up from the mouth of the canyon. From the quarry, hike to the steppy cliff band directly across canyon from Providence Falls (10–15 minutes).

The Climb: A series of short thin tiers off steppy rock bands.

Descent: Rappel or hike off.

16. PROVIDENCE FALLS A.K.A. LET PROVIDENCE GUIDE US (WI2–3, I)

Length: 100–150 feet.

Approach: This route lies in a side canyon just beyond the quarry on the south side. Approach time is 20 minutes from the quarry.

The Climb: An apron (often snow-covered) leads up to 30–40 feet of 70- to 80-degree ice.

Descent: There are small trees to rappel from. Also it's quite possible to downclimb an easy chimney (5.0) to the right of the crux, then downclimb the apron.

BLACKSMITH FORK

17. URBAN HAZE (WI2, I)

Length: Up to 800 feet.

Approach: From US 89 follow the signs to Hyrum. Stay on Utah 101 and at milepost 8.2 park at the old Civilian Conservation Corps camp in the mouth of the canyon. Hike around the fence and cross the stream into an erosion gully on the south slope; 15 minutes.

The Climb: This route consists of dirty gully ice and short bulges. It looks disgusting from the road but can actually be quite enjoyable if the ice is thick.

Descent: Hike down game trails to the east of the top of the gully.

The Northern Wasatch:

Cutler Dam to North Ogden Divide

This area of northern Utah has seen little ice climbing in spite of the fact that there is an obvious potential for more routes. The remoteness and sheer difficulty of navigating many of the canyons, especially in the mountains north of Brigham City and east of Willard, make exploring for ice more of an annoyance than most climbers are willing to undertake. Even so, some nice routes have been climbed. In fact, Willard Canyon Falls is one of Utah's most frequently climbed ice routes.

Climbing history: Little is known about the earliest ascents in the Willard area. The main falls in Willard Canyon were probably first climbed by Ogden climbers in the very late 1960s, very likely by Bruce Roghaar and a partner. At about that same time Roghaar is believed to have made the first ascent of *The Dirty Black Streak*. Undoubtedly, much of the ice in Holmes and Pearson Canyons below London Spire and Birdie's Wall was done during winter attempts on both crags in the late 1960s, 1970s, and early 1980s, but virtually no records exist. In the 1984-85 season Dave Black discovered and climbed a cluster of routes called "The Numbers" in a canyon above south Willard, and 14 years later he and Don Roberts worked out the elusive routes north of Rice Canyon near North Ogden Divide.

Getting there: Serious climbers will want to stage out of Ogden, which lies about 30 miles north of Salt Lake City near a junction of important highways: Interstate 15, I-84 (to I-80), and US 89. Approaches to routes are easily reached via U.S. Highway 89 or I-15. I-15 parallels the west slope of the Wasatch Range to its northern tip.

General Description: With the exception of Cutler Dam, the routes are located high in the canyons on the west slope of the Wasatch. Access to routes in the Cutler and Willard Canyon area are not difficult, but the routes between Willard Canyon and North Ogden Divide are in remote settings and require long and often dangerous approaches. The routes described here are from 50 to several hundred feet in length, generally over limestone or quartzite. Climbers should carry some rock gear in addition to a typical ice rack and webbing for v-threads. There are very few bolts, and most of them are old. The climbs in the slot-like canyons below the Willard Spires run over water-smoothed bedrock and are difficult to protect. Always wear a helmet.

CUTLER DAM TO NORTH OGDEN DIVIDE

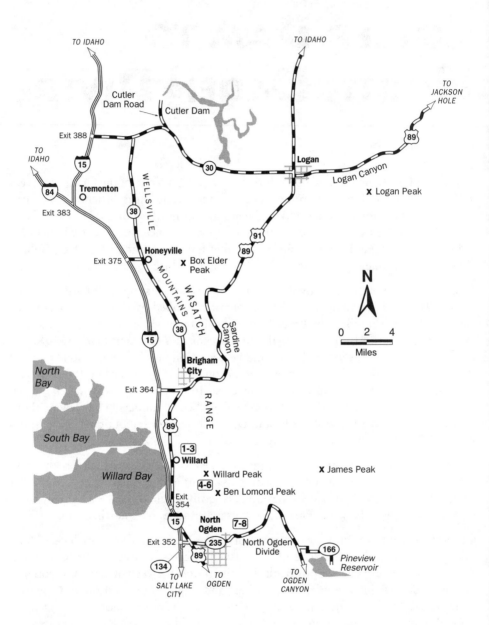

Birdies Wall *(left) and* London Spire. DAVE BLACK PHOTO

Climbing season: Like other areas along the Wasatch, the season is variable. The Willard ice generally forms up by mid-December. The Numbers tend to have a very narrow window: late December to early January.

Ethics and access: Most of the routes either lie on, or are accessed through, private property. The lack of horror stories doesn't mean there are no access problems. Utah Power and Light has been known to roust climbers from the Cutler Dam routes. As the town of Willard continues to grow and expand toward the canyons, access issues are inevitable. Climbers need to do everything within their power to maintain a healthy relationship with landowners.

Maps: USGS: Cutler Dam; Honeyville; Brigham City; Willard; Mantua; North Ogden.

Other guidebooks: None available.

Gear and guides: There are three climbing shops in the Ogden area. The shop in Smith and Edwards is very convenient to climbers in the Willard area. See Appendix B for locations and telephone numbers. Inquire at the local shops regarding guides.

Camping and accommodations: There are numerous fee and non-fee camping areas in the canyons of the Wasatch. The Wasatch "corridor" is a giant city extending from Brigham City to Spanish Fork and there is no lack of motels, bed and breakfasts, and commercial camping establishments.

Services: All services are available in Ogden and Brigham City. Willard is small. Gas is available, but get your groceries in Brigham or Ogden.

Emergency services: Call 911 for emergencies. Cell phones will work at the mouths of most of the canyons. There are two major hospitals in Ogden and one in Brigham City. Most of this area lies in Box Elder County. The county's technical winter rescue resources and capabilities are limited. If you have an emergency in the Willard Spires, be very specific about the technical and remote nature of the situation and strongly recommend assistance from the Mountain Rescue Association team from Weber County. These canyons are avalanche generators and collectors. Get a forecast (see Appendix C).

Nearby climbing and skiing: There is excellent ice climbing in the Logan, Ogden, and Salt Lake City areas. Ben Lomond Peak is a frequent target for backcountry skiers, and the south face is prized as an extreme descent. Commercial skiing is available above Ogden Valley at Nordic Valley, Powder Mountain, and Snowbasin.

CUTLER DAM

Cutler Dam is located about 15 miles west of Logan off Utah 30. Park near the base of the falls, near a bridge just south of the power station. The two obscure routes at Cutler Dam are located on property owned by Utah Power and Light. The property is posted, and permission to climb should be petitioned from UP&L. **DO NOT CLIMB WITHOUT PERMISSION.** The first route is located near the bridge, and is a 70- to 80-foot manmade falls (WI3; rappel from trees or hike around). The second route is a half-pitch on the dam spillway. It's usually thin, but an occasional structural feature can sometimes be runnered for protection.

THE WELLSVILLE MOUNTAINS

- South of Crystal Springs and east of Honeyville are several rugged canyons which inconsistently contain some climbable ice. Most of the ice that was done here in the late 1960s was on flows and seeps from the gray limestone or on verglas/mixed over quartzite slabs. As of this writing the author is unaware of additional routes in the area.

- Above the northeast end of Brigham City, just south of the gravel pit, is a small quartzite crag split by a drainage (*BC Waterfall*, WI2, half a ropelength).

WILLARD CANYON

1. WILLARD CANYON FALLS (WI2–3, II)

Length: About 800 feet (including a long WI1/snow slog).

Approach: At the old Willard cemetery (and the stone spillway) on the north end of town, drive east a half-mile, taking the right fork. From the end of the road, hike across the stream and follow a steep track on the north slope as it diagonals up east and merges with an old 4WD road at the mouth of the canyon. A trail from here crosses the stream twice before it zigzags up the south slope to the base of the climb. Time: 60–90 minutes from the parking area.

The Climb: Ascend the obvious gully for a couple of WI2 pitches. Follow a ravine that twists to the south hundred yards (WI1 with occasional bumps), a to the base of a hidden, 2-tiered 60- to 70-degree crux.

Descent: Continue another 20 yards or so above the crux, then traverse left across open slopes toward the top of Route 2 *(The Dirty Black Streak)*. This traverse has serious avalanche potential, and a slip would take the climber right over the cliffband. Some large avalanches have been witnessed both on the route and on the descent traverse. From near the top of Route 2, drop back down west and south. Follow the Youth Conservation Corp's (YCC) trail down to the base of the climb.

2. THE DIRTY BLACK STREAK (WI3–4, II)

Length: 300 feet.

Approach: From the Youth Conservation Corps trail (as described in Route 3) work your way into the shallow drainage left (north) of the main falls. Continue upward to the base of the cliff, at the bottom of the big dark "streak." This approach may require considerable bushwhacking. Time: 60–90 minutes from the parking area.

The Climb: Ascend thin ice over steps and a few steep bulges to the rim.

Descent: From the top of the climb work right (south) to the YCC trail and follow it to the base of Route 1.

3. UNNAMED (WI4, I)

Length: 90 feet.

Brian Cabe on Willard Canyon Falls. MELANIE MANSFIELD PHOTO—BRIAN CABE COLLECTION

Approach: Hike up the same trail described for Route 1, but continue up the main canyon drainage instead of ascending the south slope. Go through a narrows. The climb is located to the right (south). Time: 60–90 minutes.

The Climb: Ascend steppy, near-vertical ice to an overhang. Climb around either side.

Descent: Rappel.

WILLARD PEAK

The main approach routes to the bases of London Spire and Birdie's Wall are in Pearson and Holmes Canyons. Each has ice in the streambed, and some contrived routes can be pieced together. *Birdie's Wall Gully* (WI2) is 1 to 2 pitches in length with a 60-degree crux and is located low in Holmes Canyon.

The Numbers are a concentration of diverse climbs that feed into a narrowed upper right fork of the canyon below the north side of The Ogre. The routes are 60 to 330 feet in length. Only those over a half-pitch in length are described here. The approach is very rugged, and the entire area is prone to avalanche.

4. NUMBER 1 (WI2–4, III)

Length: About 800 feet, much of it on snow.

Approach: Drive east on 7425 South in Willard to road's end. The northeasterly hike between the road and the mouth of the canyon is on private land. Get permission to cross it. Once in the canyon, either follow the bed of the stream (cluttered with boulders, narrows, boulder moves, holes). Many climbers find it easier to stay in the streambed for a quarter-mile, then avoid the worst obstacles by ascending the north slope into the talus and cliffs for a long traverse into the canyon near the base of the route. Time: 60–90 minutes.

The Climb: Go directly up an obvious avalanche chute on the south slope. Climb over hardened avalanche debris, mixed scoured rock, and short ice bulges to a steep 60- to 70-foot crux in an overhanging corner on the left side of the gully. If the gully is not deeply buried with snow there will often be a thin but excellent rope-length WI4 smear about 50 feet to the right of the overhanging corner.

Descent: Rappel and downclimb. V-threads or bollards might be required.

5. NUMBER 2 (WI2, I–II)

Length: 200 feet.

Approach: From the vicinity of Route 4, continue hiking up the canyon, staying to the right. This route forms on the obvious water-worn rock stairway that blocks access to the upper regions of the canyon.

The Ogre

Number 1

Number 1 *is located immediately behind the large buttress low in the canyon.* The Ogre *can be seen on the skyline.* DAVE BLACK PHOTO

The Climb: Climb four large bulges to the rim. The ice is usually very thin, essentially a half-inch crust over wet rock with little or no protection.

Descent: Rappel the route (small boulder, bushes, etc.). There is rumor of a set of bolts near the lip. The route has also been downclimbed.

Note: There is a dangerous tendency to view this route as a ropeless approach to the upper routes. In 1990 this was the scene of a spectacular rim-to-base fall resulting from the ice detaching en masse. The injured climber was able to extricate himself from the canyon in three hours despite having sustained two fractures to his spine. A "proper" rescue from the outside would have been very hazardous and could have taken days.

6. NUMBER 3 (WI4–5, III)

Length: 330 feet.

Approach: The base of this climb is 25 yards up-canyon from the top of Route 5, on the north wall.

The Climb: Climb about 300 feet on very thin ice (or mixed) over low-angle water-smoothed rock. This apron is very run-out and very difficult to protect. Future parties should consider placing a bolt. At the top of the apron is a two-tiered 35-foot curtain/column crux.

Descent: Cautious and creative rappelling. There are a few bushes on top of the crux. The lower section has been downclimbed.

NORTH OGDEN DIVIDE

The following routes are located on a large cliffband high in the drainage that feeds a slot-like canyon just south of Rice Canyon (marked on USGS topo) above North Ogden.

7. ROPE DRAG NIGHTMARE (WI2 OR EASY MIXED, I–II)

Length: 300 feet.

Approach: Heading east on the Divide Road (called North Ogden Canyon Road in DeLorme's atlas), park at a pullout about 100 yards beyond the yellow "Snow Tires Required" sign. To the north is a small, slot-like canyon with a rocky notch at its mouth. Go up this canyon and into a large bowl beneath the cliffband. These routes are located on the cliffs above and right (south) of the center of the drainage. Time: 2 hours.

The Climb: Start in a left-facing dihedral and follow it 2 pitches to the rim.

Descent: Rappel the route.

8. ST. VALENTINE'S DAY MASSACRE (WI5, II)

Length: 300 feet.

Approach: From the base of *Rope Drag,* walk south 50 yards around a corner to the base of this route.

The Climb: Ascend a moderately-angled "bowl" to an intimidating, thin, vertical crux on a very run-out face.

Descent: Rappel from the top of *Rope Drag Nightmare.*

Farther up the Divide Road (North Ogden Canyon Road), high on the south-facing slope is a series of low to moderately angled quartzite crags that are frequently iced over. No data is available.

THE NORTHERN WASATCH:

NORTH OGDEN DIVIDE TO WEBER CANYON

The Ogden area is one of the most under-appreciated climbing areas in the state. The long quartzite routes of the Willard Spires and Macabre Wall are fine rock climbs, and *Malan's Waterfall* and *The Great Amphitheater Gully* are classic ice. Ogden climbers enjoy some truly good climbing and rarely find themselves having to spend a cold morning waiting for crowds like those in Little Cottonwood or Provo Canyons. Ogden is also a gateway to some of Utah's best commercial and backcountry skiing.

The city of Ogden is located on the west slope of the Wasatch Range about 35 miles north of Salt Lake City. From a historical perspective it's one of Utah's most colorful cities. Originally it was a rendezvous site for fur traders and Indians. About 130 years ago Ogden became a major junction of railways and highways. Anyone traveling east or west was bound to go through Ogden, and the city catered to the transient outsiders with bars, flophouses, dancehalls, and houses of prostitution. Some nice transformations have taken place, and the city's infamous 25th Street has been turned into a collection of cozy restaurants and upbeat shops.

Climbing history: Ice was being climbed in Ogden Canyon as early as the mid-1960s. The earliest ascents of the pipeline gullies occurred in the late 1960s, probably by the Lowes, Bruce Roghaar, Frank Cunningham, John Moore, and Paul Wilcox. Greg Lowe made several important ascents during the late 1960s and early 1970s, including *Malan's Waterfall* and *Ogden Canyon Falls*. Jeff Lowe and Bruce Roghaar climbed *The Great Amphitheater Gully* in the winter of 1972-73. Other climbers putting up new routes in the area during the 1970s included Mike Lowe and Kent Christensen. Unusual weather conditions and new pipeline leaks in the early- to mid-1980s produced a bumper crop of new climbs.

Getting there: Ogden is served by Interstate 15, I-84, and U.S. Highway 89.

General Description: The ice climbs described in this section range in length from 50 to 600 feet and form over quartzite and gneiss. Altitudes range from 4,500 to 9,000 feet. While *Malan's Waterfall* forms with some consistency, the remainder of the routes given here are less than reliable. Inversions are common, and climbs frequently

41

NORTH OGDEN DIVIDE TO WEBER CANYON

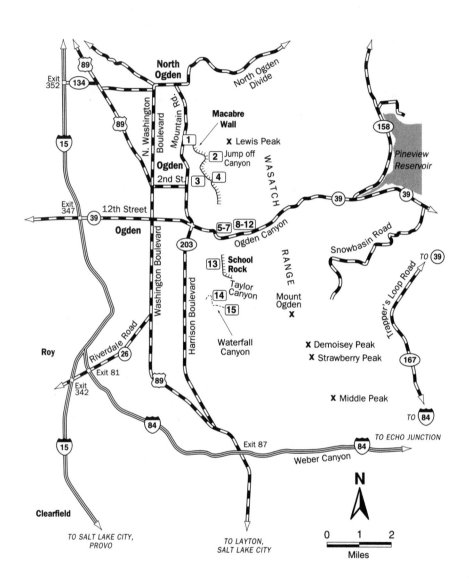

David Black on the first ascent of Sell My Gear. BLAIR KOOISTRA PHOTO,
COURTESY OGDEN STANDARD EXAMINER

melt out or do not form because of them. With a few exceptions, the "fat" routes are poorly protected from the sun and afternoon disintegration of the ice is not uncommon. Always wear a helmet.

Climbing season: There is no clear season here. Mid-winter definitely holds the best chance for the most ice. In a good year *Malan's Waterfall* can be in fat shape by very late November. *The Great Amphitheater Gully,* which faces west in clear view of the sun, has been climbed in fat conditions as late as early April.

Ethics and access: Be conservative about bolts. There are plenty of die-hard climbers here who can't understand why out-of-towners are slamming in bolts and chains when the descents are easy downclimbs or where less permanent anchor alternatives exist. Ogden has its share of access problems. The city has posted Ogden Canyon Falls and there have been some reports of climbers being hassled there and even arrested. Some of the canyon residents are very unfriendly toward climbers.

Maps: North Ogden; Ogden; Snow Basin; Devil's Slide; Henefer; Coalville.

Other guidebooks: No current guidebooks are available to ice climbs in the Ogden area. Mecham's *Ogden Rock Climbs* is available in local shops, and a more comprehensive area guidebook is in the works.

Gear and guides: There are three excellent climbing shops in Ogden: Black Diamond, Canyon Sports, and Smith and Edwards. See Appendix B for addresses and numbers. For decades there have been a handful of "pirate" guides operating in the area. Exum Utah Mountain Adventures currently has the only permit to guide climbs on a regular basis in the Wasatch-Cache National Forest.

Camping and accommodations: There are limitless hotels and motels in Ogden, with a major concentration along the freeway corridor. Several commercial campgrounds operate in Ogden and Ogden Valley (east of the city). Most Forest Service campgrounds are either closed for the winter or snowed in. Car camping in or near the city or in Ogden Canyon is not recommended, except in developed campgrounds.

Services: A huge, sprawling city runs from Ogden to Provo, with Salt Lake City in the middle. There is no lack of services of any type.

Emergency services: Call 911 for all emergencies. Weber County has a Mountain Rescue Association team staffed with some top-notch climbers. There are two major hospitals in the Ogden area. For avalanche conditions call the forecast center (Appendix C).

Nearby climbing and skiing: There is excellent ice in the Cottonwood Canyons above Salt Lake City. Little Cottonwood Canyon has first-rate granite climbing. Ogden Canyon sports a few crags that are not yet closed to climbers, but most of the easily accessed rock in the canyon is off limits. School Rock and Macabre Wall are large west-facing crags just above the city. The boulderfield above 26th Street is exceptional. They are a good alternative when the weather is too warm for stable ice.

In anticipation of the 2002 Olympics, Snowbasin has undergone incredible expansion and improvement. Its upper bowls are a superb place to ski. Adjacent to the area and within a short ski of the lifts and trams are some enjoyable rock climbs (e.g., the northeast face of Mount Ogden). Other ski areas within 30 minutes of Ogden are Nordic Valley and Powder Mountain. North Fork Park, in Ogden Valley, is a good place to backcountry ski. The nearby Culter Ridge route to the top of Mount Ben Lomond is popular with local ski mountaineers, and the South Face of Ben Lomond Peak is a draw to extreme skiers.

LEWIS PEAK SECTION

1. GNEISS-N-ICY (WI2, I)

Length: 165 feet.

Approach: This route is located in a gully/left dihedral on the left side of Macabre Wall. When it's "in," it can be seen from Harrison Boulevard. To find it, take 12th Street and turn north on Harrison Boulevard. Follow it to any convenient location beneath Macabre Wall, north of Jump Off Canyon. A lot of new housing is being built in this area, and there are plenty of No Trespassing signs. Work your way around them and hike up to the dark brown gneiss crag directly below the south end of Macabre Wall. Time: 30 minutes.

The Climb: Ascend a low-angle gully, a 15-foot icicle, and a series of short, easy steps.

Descent: Hike off to the north or south.

2. JUMP OFF CANYON FALLS (WI3–4, I)

Length: 200 feet or more.

Approach: The climb is located high in the east corner of the south slope of this box canyon. Hike directly up the large canyon to the south of Macabre Wall. Time: 60–90 minutes.

The Climb: Greg Lowe describes this as "a mellow climb with a steep final pitch." It rarely forms.

Descent: Rappel.

3. FIREMAN'S NOTCH (WI2–3, I)

Length: 100 feet.

Approach: From the northern end of Polk Avenue (and north of 150 South) hike up the bottom of a shallow canyon east to the base of a smooth wall. Time: 30 minutes.

The Climb: Climb directly up the smooth wall, 60 to 70 degrees. The ice is usually very thin and difficult to protect.

Descent: Rappel the route or hike around to the north or south.

4. THE GREAT AMPHITHEATER GULLY (WI3, II–III) ★

Length: 600 feet.

Approach: Park on the east end of Third Street or Douglas Avenue and hike east into the obvious wide gully. 90 minutes. The climb is more distant than it appears and it's very difficult to determine conditions from the road without a good pair of binoculars or a spotting scope. Look for it to form when warm thaws are followed by frigid temperatures. Because of its western aspect, it melts out quickly.

The Climb: This is a fine, classic gully when fat; when thin it is an exciting, moderate mixed climb that is well protected with rock gear. After conquering a 15-foot icicle or step, climb directly upward over consistently moderate ice or mixed for 4 or 5 pitches to the rim. A great route.

Descent: Rappel the length of the gully, to the south of the climb. The rock is very broken here and climbers should be very suspicious of the old pitons, some of which have been there for 40 years. It is possible to avoid this rappel by a long strenuous hike to the next deep canyon to the south.

OGDEN CANYON

The following routes are located in Ogden Canyon and are approached by driving east on 12th Street to the mouth of Ogden Canyon. Park either at Rainbow Gardens on the south side of the highway just below the mouth, or at a pullout directly below Ogden Canyon Falls. Route 5 is located on the north wall of the canyon, just west of where the stream drops beneath the road and switches sides. Routes 6 through 12 are also located on the north slope, but east of the drop.

What was a top-notch concentration of easily reached climbs was virtually eliminated by pipeline reconstruction in the early 1990s. At this writing, the only routes that form up with any consistency are the standard and variation routes of the main falls. However, in the 1998–1999 season *Gully II* was briefly climbable, and in the 1999–2000 season *Shit for Brains, Three Steps,* all three of the *Gully* routes, and *FLF* had thin ice. It appears that naturally or otherwise these climbs are on their way to recovery.

5. SHIT FOR BRAINS (WI3–4, I)

Length: 80–200 feet.

Approach: From the pullout beneath the main falls, walk a few yards to the west end of the guard rail and start climbing.

The Climb: The route follows a steep, thin flow on the broken rock. From the rim of the cliff continue on low-angle ice or snow to the pipeline.

Descent: Hike down along trails to the west.

6. OGDEN CANYON FALLS (WI4–5, I)

Length: 250 feet.

Approach: From the pullout below the falls, cross the bridge and make an unpleasant scrambling traverse left to the base of the falls where it drops into the river. Time: 15 minutes.

The Climb: About 200 feet of moderately angled ice leads to the base of a 40-foot column. Climb it to the pipeline.

Descent: Hike down along trails to the west.

VARIATION: There are two major variations. The first is a narrow gully on the left that merges with the main flow midway between the river and the column. The second variation is *Ogden Canyon Falls Right,* which is a longer, exposed climb over thin ice on the large, steep wall to the right of the column.

7. SELL MY GEAR AND BUY A VCR (WI5, I)

Length: 400 feet.

Approach: This rarely forming column climb is on the far left end of the overhanging rock climbing crag known as The Gneiss Wall, 100 feet to the right of the base of the main falls. Approach as for the main falls. If the river is too high, it's possible to hike up a talus slope directly above the bridge and to the right of The Gneiss Wall, then scramble to the west into the gully, directly above the column. Rappel to the base of the column. The bolt there is old and very questionable.

The Climb: Ascend a 120-foot vertical column to the rim of the gneiss. Continue a few pitches over low-angle ice or snow and two short curtains to the pipeline.

Descent: From the pipeline, hike to the west, or from the gully above the column, traverse east to a talus slope that drops down to the bridge.

8. THREE STEPS BUTTRESS (WI2–5, I)

Length: 200 feet.

Approach: From the pullout below the main falls, cross the bridge and walk along a service road about 10 minutes to a large gneiss buttress.

The Climb: *Three Steps* is the ramp on the left (west) side of the crag. The route climbs 2 easy pitches of bulges, then either moves right into an easy corner, or farther up the ramp to the base of a curtain of icicles ranging from 20 feet in length on the right to 60 feet on the left. Continue up to the pipeline on easy ice and snow.

Descent: Hike west along the pipeline and drop down the scree gully to the west of the crag.

9. GULLY I (WI3, I)

Length: 200 feet.

Approach: This is located about 10 yards to the east of the base of Route 8. It's barely recognizable as a gully and may occasionally form on the face adjacent to Route 10.

The Climb: The start varies. It may merge with Route 10 at its base or drop directly off overhangs to the left. Follow a series of steps to the pipeline.

Descent: Follow the pipeline west and drop down the scree gully.

10. GULLY II (WI2–3, I)

Length: 300 feet.

Approach: Start over a steep double step (35 feet) and follow the gully to a runnered flake (belay/rappel). The second pitch veers right for 90 feet. A final pitch goes up and left over bulges through rocks and junipers to the pipeline.

Descent: Follow the pipeline to the east a few hundred yards, then drop down a scree gully. Be cautious. There are cliffs below this traverse and it's been the site of several near tragedies.

11. GULLY III (WI2–3, I)

Length: 230 feet.

Approach: Approach as for Route 8. This is the notch located several yards to the east of the base of Route 10.

The Climb: Ascend a steep 35-foot step. Continue through the notch and up the gully. Eventually move left and merge with the second or third pitch of Route 10.

Descent: At the pipeline, traverse east until a scree slope to the service road is reached.

12. FLF (WI4–5, I)

Length: 230 feet.

Approach: This route is located on the vertical and overhanging walls about 100 feet to the right of Route 11.

The Climb: Ascend a 30-foot vertical step, a short ramp, and another 30-foot vertical step (bolts) into a shallow notch. Continue to the pipeline on progressively easier ice.

Dave Black on Gully II *in 1981.* PAT PALMIERI PHOTO

Descent: Hike east and down a scree slope, or from the top of the first pitch (crux), rappel from bolts or hike east.

MOUNT OGDEN—NORTHEAST FACE

The northeast face of Mount Ogden has been described in at least one book as a classic ice route. As of this writing no extensive ice has been seen on the face since at least 1980. However, this face does make an excellent mixed snow and rock climb (5.7, several pitches). With the expansive new lift system at Snowbasin, the face is very easy to access. Even with improved avalanche control in the bowls there is a constant danger of slides beneath this face. In the spring, hidden in the snow below the face, there may be several glide cracks large enough to eat a climber. Before approaching this climb, get an avalanche forecast and check in with the ski patrol. Forest Service closures are there for your protection and there are stiff fines for ignoring them.

EAST BENCH ROUTES

13. SCHOOL ROCK (WI3–4, I)

Length: Up to 330 feet.

Approach: From the top of 26th Street, hike through brush and talus to the middle of the base of the large quartzite cliff band just north of Taylor Canyon. Time: 45 minutes.

The Climb: Climb steep steps to some wide ledges, then work up a steep corner to the rim of the cliff. This final pitch rarely gets much ice.

Descent: Rappel the route, or traverse north and hike around.

14. FROSTED FLAKES (WI1–2, I)

Length: Up to 650 feet.

Approach: From the top of 29th Street, take the trail to Waterfall Canyon. Midway between 29th Street and Waterfall Canyon, head up into some low-angle quartzite crags. Time: 20 minutes.

The Climb: In a web of low-angle gullies, weave through the rocks. This route is a long exercise in flat-footing. It rarely forms and is usually hidden beneath snow.

Descent: Hike down adjacent slopes.

15. MALAN'S WATERFALL (WI5, II) ★

Length: Up to 310 feet.

Greg Lowe on Malan's Waterfall, *circa 1971.* Lowe Collection

Approach: Although climbers frequently park at the end of 32nd Street and hike across the golf course, the standard approach is done from the trailhead at the east end of 29th Street. Ascend the mountainside on a trail that heads south to Waterfall Canyon. In the mouth of the canyon, cross a small bridge and head east into the canyon. Follow the trail along the north side of the stream until the base of the falls is reached. Time: 60 minutes.

The Climb: This ice has a southerly aspect, so early starts are a necessity and cold, cloudy days are a blessing. Many climbers have had humbling brushes with death when the upper pitch has collapsed and exploded into an avalanche of ice dust and killer chunks. The standard route ascends the far right side and is the safest line on the flow. Climb a full pitch of steep ice (150 feet) to a wide ledge, where there is a small runnered tree and some bolts. The second pitch follows the corner, then traverses left to the base of the 45-foot crux column or a shorter cauliflower cone variation to its right. Both these features are usually thin, hollow, and quite intimidating. It's also possible to set up a belay in an alcove to the right of the base of these features. The crux pitch ends in a large, flat alcove. At the back of the alcove, a final pitch over a 50-foot bulge leads to a wide gully. The more direct left side variations of the first two pitches are consistently near-vertical and exposed to ice falling from the column and cone. Some protection can be gained in a belay alcove on the left margin.

Descent: Descend in two 2-rope rappels from fixed anchors on the right (east) side. It's also possible to hike 200 yards up the gully, then traverse right over a ridge and onto a slope that narrows into the chute 200 feet to the right of the base of the falls.

The Central Wasatch:

The Cottonwood Canyons

The Salt Lake City area should certainly be on a "Ten Best Places in America for Climbers to Live" list. Endless and immediately accessible alpine settings on 11,000-foot glacier-scoured peaks, wilderness areas and national forests, awesome backcountry ski terrain, fine commercial ski areas, perfect powder snow, roadside multipitch climbing on soaring granite and quartzite walls, an enormous offering of cultural and educational niceties—what else is needed?

Climbing history: There have been so many people climbing ice in the Cottonwoods for so many generations that it's difficult to define the first ascensionists of many of the routes. The earliest and historically most important ascent of a major water ice climb in Utah was Ted Wilson's and Rick Reese's 1960s step-cutting ascent of the *The Great White Icicle*. It and *Stairway to Heaven* (Provo Canyon) are now the two most popular and crowded ice climbs in the state. Dave George and George Lowe did the first ice ascent of *Super Slab* in the late 1960s. In Big Cottonwood Canyon, Dave Jenkins and Rick Wyatt climbed *Storm Mountain Falls* in 1979. *Scottish Gully* was climbed by Brett Ruckman and Gary Olsen in the early 1980s.

Getting there: If coming on Interstate 15 from the south, take exit 302 onto I-215, which goes east and will eventually head north. Get off on exit 7 (6200 South). If coming on I-15 from the north, take exit 307 onto I-80 east and connect with I-215 heading south, then take exit 6 (6200 South).

After taking exit 6 or exit 7 off I-215, follow the signs south to a traffic light at 7200 South. Turn east for Big Cottonwood Canyon. To get to Little Cottonwood, continue south and follow the signs to Snowbird and Alta.

General Description: The routes described here range from 110 to 1,000 feet in length and sit at altitudes from 5,000 to 11,000 feet, forming over quartzite and gneiss in Big Cottonwood and granite (actually quartz monzonite) in Little Cottonwood. A standard rack of screws and a few pieces of rock pro will do for most of these routes in fat conditions. Take more rock pro when things are thin, especially in Big Cottonwood. Helmets and protective eyewear are highly recommended. You WILL get hit on *The Great White Icicle* because of the crowds, even if your party is the first on the

BIG AND LITTLE COTTONWOOD CANYONS

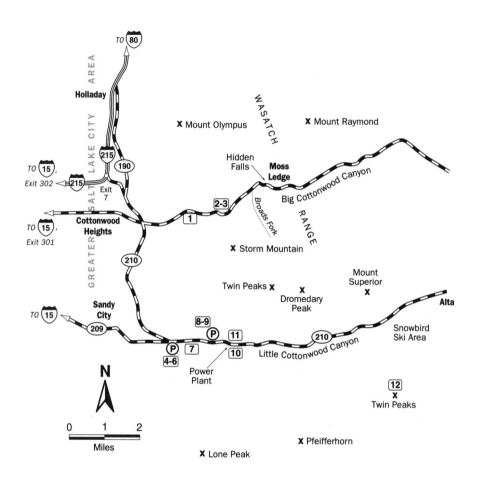

ice that day. Many climbers do solo repetitions and they dislodge a lot of ice as they cruise past roped parties.

Climbing season: The fat routes in Little Cottonwood (*Scruffy* and *Great White*) are usually in shape by mid-December. *The Great White Icicle* may stay fat until late February or early March if the weather cooperates. Inversions frequently melt out the first and last pitches of *The Great White Icicle*. The thinner routes like those in Big Cottonwood are usually quite sparse and can be gone in the blink of an eye during inversions or rains.

Ethics and access: In Big Cottonwood there are very few access problems. Probably the biggest access headache is finding a place to park. When you do find a place to park, watch out: The plows are not shy about walling you in. The situation in Little Cottonwood is similar. The power plant pullout has room for six to ten vehicles. On weekends, go early if you want a space. Farther up the canyon, parking becomes an avalanche hazard issue. There are several active slide paths and you can be ticketed for stopping or parking. The Latter Day Saint (Mormon) Church owns much of the north side granite and some of the property is posted.

Maps: USGS: Dromedary Peak; Draper; Mt. Aire.

Guidebooks: There are a number of guidebooks to the rock climbs of the area (see Appendix B). Andrew McClean's book *The Chuting Gallery* is a guide to steep skiing in the Wasatch and describes some of the gullies that are popular snow climbs in the late spring and early summer.

Gear and guides: There are a half-dozen excellent climbing shops in Salt Lake City, including Black Diamond, REI, International Mountain Equipment and Wasatch Touring. For guide services, check with Exum (Appendix B) and ask around at the climbing shops.

Camping and accommodations: With the parking and avalanche problems up in the canyons, and with so many inexpensive hotels and motels down in Salt Lake City, it doesn't make sense to try to camp. The farther away from the canyons you sleep and eat, the less it will cost. Doesn't everyone have an old climbing buddy who lives in Salt Lake City? Stay there.

Services: This is a major metropolitan area and has the state's largest selection of services of all types. Unlike Provo, Salt Lake City doesn't shut down on Sunday.

Emergency services: Call 911 for all emergencies. There are a half-dozen major hospitals and many large clinics and smaller hospitals in the Salt Lake Valley. There are also two major helicopter medevac services that routinely operate in the Wasatch Mountains and work closely with the local search-and-rescue agencies. Salt Lake County search and rescue has excellent technical capabilities and is one of the busiest Mountain Rescue Association units in the country. Always get an avalanche and weather forecast before climbing in the Cottonwoods (see Appendix C).

Elaine Holland leading The Great White Icicle. *Bruce Bidner soloing below.* BRIAN CABE PHOTO

Nearby climbing and skiing: Salt Lake City is centrally located within an hour of the major resorts, including Snowbasin, Alta, Snowbird, Park City, Brighton, Solitude, Deer Valley, The Canyons, Sundance, and Powder Mountain. This area attracts and retains a large and dedicated group of ski mountaineers and free-heel skiers. Excellent ice climbing is found in Ogden to the north and Provo to the south.

BIG COTTONWOOD CANYON

1. SCOTTISH GULLY (WI4, M4, I)

Length: 260 feet.

Approach: Look for a geologic site sign on the south side of the road about 2.5 miles up the canyon. Park there at the pullout and walk to the west edge of a buttress known as the JBOH Wall. Hike up the wide gully, past some large trees, to the base of a small alcove. Time: 5 minutes.

The Climb: Ascend a 20-foot icicle into the narrow gully above and follow thin ice or mixed rock and ice for 2 pitches. Bring a good selection of rock gear.

Descent: Rappel the route.

2. STORM MOUNTAIN FALLS (WI4–5, I)

Length: 270 feet.

Approach: Park at or near the Storm Mountain picnic area. It's usually gated and blocked by snow, but east around a bend there's a pullout. A 10-minute hike will put you at the base of the route.

The Climb: Climb WI4–5 drips over the tilted strata for 80 feet to bolts on the right. The second pitch ascends WI3 left-trending slabs to fixed pitons below a 20-foot icicle in an overhung corner. Climb the icicle and continue up to a large boulder. An M4 variation forms a few yards to the left of the first pitch. Another thin smear drops into the slabby gully about 50 feet to the left of the main route.

Descent: Rappel the route (two ropes).

3. B-PITCH (WI4, I)

Length: 180 feet.

Approach: This occasionally forms on a wall called the Bumble Bee Wall (see photo), which is located northwest of the picnic area and about 150 feet left of Route 2.

The Climb: Three steps. Expect some mixed climbing.

Descent: Rappel the route, or from the top of the wall it's possible to downclimb west and hike around.

Storm Mountain Falls *in lean conditions.* The Bumble Bee Wall *is seen in the lower left.* DAVE BLACK PHOTO

Broads Fork Icefall (WI3–5) is a 50-foot route located high up Broads Fork about 2.5 miles from Utah 190. There are also several substantial flows that form up on the north side of the canyon between Hidden Falls/North Mill B and Moss Ledge about 4.5 to 5 miles from the mouth of the canyon. As of this writing, the author has not found reliable information regarding routes on these flows.

LITTLE COTTONWOOD CANYON

4. SCRUFFY RIGHT (WI4, I)

Length: 200 feet.

Approach: Scruffy Band is the first granite crag on the south side of the canyon. To approach, take the Temple Quarry Nature Trail road just south of the junction of Utah 209 and UT 210. From the parking area, follow a trail east a few hundred feet to a footbridge over the stream. Cross the bridge and hike up to the base of the route. Time: 20 minutes.

The Climb: This is the westernmost of the flows, located about 30 feet west of Route 5. Climb a WI4 face for 200 feet. It's usually done in a single pitch with a 60m rope but can easily be broken into 2 pitches at the snow ledge about 50 feet from the top.

Scruffy Band. *All 3 routes are clearly seen in the lower left quadrant of the photo. Left to right:* Hanging Pillar, Scruffy Band, Scruffy Right. BRIAN SMOOT PHOTO

Descent: Hike off to the east and downclimb or rappel (2 ropes) from a large tree about 60 feet to the east.

5. SCRUFFY BAND (WI3–4, I) ★

Length: 200 feet.

Approach: As described above.

The Climb: Climb a WI3 ramp to the large snow ledge. The second pitch ascends a 15-foot pillar.

Descent: Hike and downclimb to the east, or rappel from the tree.

6. HANGING PILLAR (WI5–6, I)

Length: 110 feet.

Approach: As described above.

The Climb: About 30 feet left (east) of Route 4, climb a WI3 apron to a corner leading up left to a difficult icicle. A difficult mixed variation of this route follows a bolt ladder immediately above the WI3 apron, directly up the face to the right of the icicle (*Razzleberry,* M8 or M9).

Descent: Hike and downclimb to the east or rappel from the tree.

7. SUPER SLAB (WI2–3, I–II)

Length: Up to 600 feet.

Approach: From *Scruffy Band,* hike east about 600 feet.

The Climb: Thin ice over low-angle granite slabs.

Descent: Creative rappelling and downclimbing.

8. COLD DUCK (WI3–4, I)

Length: 100 feet.

Approach: This is located in a gully about 600 feet west of *Kermit's Wall* and on the lower right (east) side of *The Waterfront,* just over a mile from the mouth of the canyon.

The Climb: This is a southeast facing climb that basically follows the same line as the rock climb *Disco Duck* to a bolt station.

Descent: Rappel.

Mel Brown on Scruffy Band. BRIAN CABE PHOTO

9. BECKY'S WALL (M5, I–II)

Length: 200 feet or more.

Approach: This is the obvious openbook directly above the Gate Buttress parking area at MM 5.1. Work up through trails and scrub oak to the base. Time: 15–20 minutes.

The Climb: Thin ice (rarely forms) over smooth slabs in a large, right-facing dihedral. Protect with rock gear. Watch for bolt stations. This is a very popular rock route (*Becky's Wall, 5.7*).

Descent: Rappel from bolts at the top of the standard rock pitches.

10. THE GREAT WHITE ICICLE (WI3, II) ★★

Length: 650 feet.

Approach: Park at a pullout at a small cement building (power plant) near the road on the south side at MM 5.7, about 2 miles from the junction of Utah 209 and UT 210. Cross the stream on a small bridge behind the building and follow a trail to the

Gate Buttress *(right) and* The Waterfront *(left center, with waterstains) in summer conditions. The big dihedral of* Becky's Wall *is on the far right.*
Dave Black photo

The Great White Icicle. DAVE BLACK PHOTO

west a few hundred feet. Keep your eyes open for a trough that cuts up the slope toward the climb and follow it to the base. Time: 20–30 minutes. Expect crowds.

The Climb: Pitch 1: Ascend a 50-foot apron to bolts on a huge chockstone on the right. Pitch 2: A long gully of snow and ice to bolts on a wide, snowy ledge to the left. Pitch 3: Climb over The Bulge (60 degrees) and up to the right beneath the crux pitch to a tight, slanted alcove and some bolts. The final pitch surmounts the 80-degree headwall. This is often a crumbling, wet, cauliflower structure. The final 15-foot column can be bypassed by climbing to the left above the big evergreen tree.

On occasion, a two-pitch variation forms to the left of The Bulge. It requires a few rock moves and exits near the large evergreen tree left of the top of the normal crux.

Descent: The most common descent from the top is by traversing west (right), usually in a very obvious trough in the snow, to a large gully that can be descended to the base of the buttress using an entertaining combination of scrambling, flat-footing, glissading, and postholing. Otherwise, rappel from bolts below the crux.

11. VANILLA ICE (WI4, 5.6, I)

Length: 300–400 feet.

Approach: From the power plant pullout at MM 5.7, cross the highway and hike northwest up a gated dirt road toward the large buttress (Black Peeler Buttress). Leave the road at the switchback and hike to the base of the route.

The Climb: This route very rarely forms, and it consists of very thin ice on the Black Peeler Buttress. It will probably require some moderate 5th-class rock climbing to get to.

Descent: Rappel and downclimb.

12. PIPELINE COULOIR, AMERICAN FORK TWIN (AI2, II–III)

Length: Up to 1,000 feet, including the bowl below (grossly shorter and possibly melted out by late summer).

Approach: The easiest way to approach this route is to take the Snowbird Tram to the top, then hike south along a road that switchbacks down around a rocky ridge and into the northeast cirque. Those not wanting to take the tram can hike up maintenance roads.

The Climb: This is a hidden couloir that ascends the northeast side of the west twin. It is frequently described as an alpine ice couloir. It's mostly metamorphosed snow—hopefully frozen—and a smattering of water ice, most of which melts out by late summer. The couloir reaches 42 degrees and is consistently near that angle. It's been a popular early summer climb for several decades.

A climber on the northeast face of Storm Mountain, *considered by many local climbers to be the classic alpine route. Normally a late-winter climb, it ascends a major gully system to the left of a large right-facing corner, then finishes on 600 feet of moderate face climbing to the summit.* BRIAN SMOOT PHOTO

Descent: From the saddle, traverse to the east twin and follow a trail back to the tram.

Note: This route brings up the question of "Alpine Ice" in Utah. There are several Wasatch peaks like the American Fork Twin that have north-aspect couloirs or cirques that may contain frozen snow and varying amounts of water ice well into summer. These include the northeast and northwest couloirs of The Pfeiferhorn, the northeast couloir of Lone Peak, Devil's Castle Couloir, the northwest couloir of Box Elder Peak, and *Grunge Couloir* and *Moving Target Couloir* on Mount Timpanogos. They may be fun midsummer hard snow routes, but none of them has the adequate angle, altitude, aspect, and enclosure combination needed to retain an ice route of any significant length all year, every year.

On the other hand, many of the higher Wasatch peaks have faces and couloirs that collect enough late fall and/or winter water ice or mixed conditions to attract a few hardy climbers. The northeast face of Storm Mountain, the north ridge and east-aspect faces of the Pfeifferhorn, Baldy Chute near Alta, and the south face of Mount Superior are good examples. Approaches to many of these routes are major undertakings and require good mountain skills and patience. Always investigate conditions and inquire at adjacent ski areas regarding closures.

Kennan Harvey on the south face of Mount Superior. CHRIS HARMSTON PHOTO

The Central Wasatch:

Mount Timpanogos and Provo Canyon

From Interstate 15, Mount Timpanogos forms a stark and imposing skyline behind the cities of Provo and Orem, 60 miles south of Salt Lake City. Now an official wilderness area, Mount Timpanogos is probably the most popular mountain in Utah. Thousands climb it each year, and, interestingly, an annual summer hiking event held until the 1970s used to put nearly 10,000 people on the mountain in a single day. In winter "Timp" becomes far more formidable, and, with the exception of skiers at Sundance, there are no crowds. The mountain hulk and the canyons surrounding Mount Timpanogos hold the largest concentration of reliable ice routes in the state. Provo Canyon is the logical destination for out-of-state climbers who want a taste of Utah's quality multipitch routes.

Climbing history: The earliest known ascent of a major ice route in Provo Canyon was Greg Lowe's solo of *Bridal Veil Falls* in 1971. In December 1975, Jim Knight and Mark Ward climbed *Stairway to Heaven*. That route is still considered by most Utah climbers to be the state's finest ice climb. In 1976, Jeff and Mike Lowe climbed *Stewart Falls,* and *The Fang* was done by Jeff Lowe, Greg Lowe, Mike Lowe, Kim Miller, and Jim Knight. *Post Nasal Drip* was climbed in 1982 by Rick Wyatt and Evelyn Lees. The first major route in American Fork, *Creamsickle,* was done in 1983 by Brian Smoot and Jim Knight. During the early to mid-1980s, the routes in Battle Creek, Lost Creek, and Rock Canyons were explored. In 1994–1995 Brian Smoot and associates climbed *Habeas Corpus* and *White Lie* in American Fork Canyon. In the late 1990s, serious mixed variations were being done on many of the old stock routes.

Getting there: From the east and northeast, U.S. Highway 40 intersects with US 189 in Heber City. From Heber City, take US 189 southwest into Provo Canyon. On the west side of the mountains, the Orem/Provo area can be reached from the north or south via I-15. To get to Provo Canyon, Sundance Ski Area, and Aspen Grove from I-15, take exit 275 and drive east on Utah 52, then take US 189 northeast into Provo Canyon. To get to American Fork Canyon from I-15, take exit 287 and follow US 92 east to American Fork Canyon and Timpanogos Cave. Watch for signs pointing the way.

MOUNT TIMPANOGOS AND PROVO CANYON

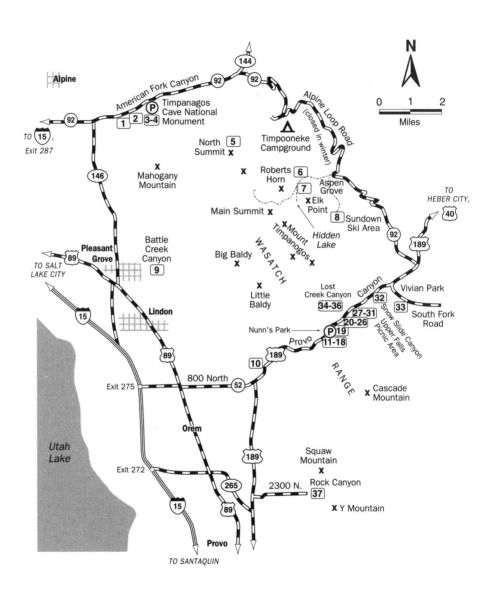

Bill Foster on White Nightmare. BRIAN CABE PHOTO

General Description: The routes described in this section range from 40 to 1,000 feet at altitudes of between 5,000 and 11,100 feet. The crags are predominantly limestone. *Stairway to Heaven* is probably the most crowded climb in the state, and queues frequently form at the bases of *The Fang, Bridal Veil,* and *Miller's Thriller.* The crowding is more than a simple annoyance: major avalanche and ice fall problems are exacerbated by the human traffic. Helmets are an absolute necessity, and all climbers are advised to carry avalanche gear (transceivers, shovels, probes) when climbing anywhere in these mountains and canyons.

Climbing season: The routes in the cirques above Aspen Grove come into shape very early in the season. It's not unusual to find fat ice there as early as October. *Grunge Couloir* is described with some reservations as an alpine ice climb, which means that in a normal snow/temperature year it might be climbed through the summer. Provo Canyon routes will typically come into shape in early December and will be good until late February.

Ethics and access: At this writing there do not seem to be any major access issues for ice climbers. Common sense and courtesy should be employed at all times in order to keep access problems at a minimum. The Alpine Loop Road between Aspen Grove and American Fork Canyon is now a fee area in both directions. Access to Stewart Falls through the Sundance residences has been a problem in the past, but there is an alternate approach, which is given in the route description.

Maps: Timpanogos Cave; Aspen Grove; Orem; Bridal Veil Falls.

Other guidebooks: No ice climbing guides specific to this area exist, although Wagner's *Utah Ice* contains some useful topos and diagrams. See Appendix A for mountaineering and rock climbing guidebooks.

Gear and guides: There are several climbing shops in Provo and Orem. See Appendix B. Check with Hansen High Adventure Specialities in Orem or Exum in Salt Lake City for information on guides and instruction.

Camping and accommodations: There are dozens of hotels and motels in the urban corridor along the west slope of Mount Timpanogos. There's a good selection of sleeping establishments in Heber City (east of Provo Canyon). There are also a number of commercial and public camping areas in the cities and in Uinta National Forest.

Services: Nearly half a million people live in and near Utah Valley, so Monday through Saturday there is no lack of services. Sunday, however, is another story. Provo-Orem is under some serious religious influence, far more so than almost any other spot in the state. On Sunday morning the city has the eerie atmosphere of one of those deserted cities in an old Twilight Zone re-run. Do not be surprised if the service is slow and cold in those few establishments that are open on the Sabbath Day.

Emergency services: Call 911 for all emergencies. Cell phones work in most locations, the exceptions being American Fork Canyon and the narrowest sections of

Provo Canyon. There are several major hospitals in the urban corridor between American Fork and Provo. Local search and rescue resources are very experienced: Mount Timpanogos is NOT a kind mountain.

Nearby climbing and skiing: Good ice is available in Santaquin Canyon, North Creek Canyon, Spanish Fork Canyon, and Diamond Fork Canyon to the south, and the Cottonwood Canyons to the north. Sundance Ski Area near Aspen Grove provides downhill and commercial nordic skiing. Backcountry skiing is popular here. Winter ascents of the Mount Timpanogos summit are a prize.

AMERICAN FORK CANYON

Several ice routes have been put up in American Fork Canyon, but the information is sketchy, and anyone interested in trying out the ice there is forewarned that there is a substantial rockfall hazard where those lines tend to form. Almost all the ice is on the south side of the canyon. In addition to the routes listed here, climbs have been done in the large drainage just east of *Drizzlepuss* (*Gemini Falls,* WI3–4, half pitch), the southside cliffs between that drainage and the power plant, and on crags across from the power plant. A long route has been done high on the east slope of Cattle Creek Canyon (*Cattle Creek Falls,* WI3–4, two pitches).

1. DRIZZLEPUSS (WI4, I)

Length: 90 feet.

Approach: This is located near the mouth of the canyon, just past the Information Center signs, on the south side, in a smoothed-out gully with a large broken buttress on the right. Cross the stream and hike to the base of the gully.

The Climb: Scramble up the gully to low-angle ice and follow it to a 50-foot, 70- to 80-degree crux finish.

Descent: Rappel the route.

2. CREAMSICKLE (WI5–6, I)

Length: 300 feet.

Approach: This is located on the south slope, about two-thirds of a mile from the mouth of the canyon. It's the first major flow of ice visible from the highway and is located about 600 feet above the canyon floor. Crossing the stream may be problematic. The first ascent party crossed on avalanche debris.

The Climb: Three pitches. Climb thin I3 slabs then mixed snow and ice to the base of a 50-foot pillar. Ascend the pillar and make a rock move onto slabby ice to a ledge.

Descent: Rappel the route from a tree to the west.

3. WHITE LIE (WI4, II)

Length: 430 feet.

Approach: This route is difficult to see from the highway. Hike up the Timpanogos Cave Trail. Where the trail is gated it may be necessary to do a few rock moves around a large boulder in order to regain the trail. About 0.25 mile beyond the gate, leave the trail and enter a gully. 1 hour.

The Climb: Three pitches. Climb an easy gully with a fixed piton midway on the left, to a belay ledge. Ascend mixed snow and thin ice to the base of a cone and 20-foot pillar. Belay beneath the roof on the right. The final pitch ascends the pillar to a snow slope.

Descent: From a tree to the right of the top of the route, rappel to the base of the cone/pillar. V-threads or screws may be needed for the rappel down the second pitch.

4. HABEAS CORPUS (WI4–5, II)

Length: 650 feet.

Approach: Continue up the Timpanogos Cave Trail through steep switchbacks to a restroom facility just east of the main trail. The climb lies in a gully just above the restroom and is visible from the trail. 1.5 hours.

The Climb: Five pitches. 60m ropes are recommended. Belay and rappel slings mark the route. Ascend a long pitch of I2 past two fixed pitons (left, then right) to a belay

A climber on the second pitch of Habeas Corpus. BRIAN SMOOT PHOTO

atop a cement retaining structure. The second pitch ascends 190 feet of snow, ice bulges, and rock moves to a belay station (two pitons and a bolt) located just below a bifurcation in the gully. Another long pitch ascends the right fork onto a snow slope to a belay station with three fixed pitons. Traverse right to a short 90-degree step. Climb it and follow easier ice above about 100 feet to two fixed pitons on a ledge to the left. The final pitch ascends thin 80–85 degree ice for about 70 feet. From the top of the ice make a long mixed traverse (5.7) to a tree.

Descent: Rappel from the tree, and continue the rappel descent along the lower belay stations.

MOUNT TIMPANOGOS, NORTH AND EAST SLOPES

5. GRUNGE COULOIR (AI2–3, III–IV)

Length: 1,000–1,200 feet.

Approach: Drive up American Fork Canyon and follow the signs to the Timpooneke Campground area. At 0.3 mile beyond the edge of the pavement, take a left turn into

The north face of Mount Timpanogos. Grunge Couloir is in the shadows on the right. Down left on the lower face of the cliffs, a long spit of water ice can be seen. This potential route continues up the gully and cliffs for hundreds of feet to just below the top of the peak.
DOUG COATS PHOTO

A closer look at Grunge Couloir. DOUG COATS PHOTO

the area marked "Timpooneke Campground Units 15–32." Park in the vicinity of Unit 17. There is a clear view of the couloir from this spot. Examine the couloir with binoculars to determine how much ice and snow remain. Some years, the ice is totally melted out by the end of August. From Campground Unit 17, it's possible to work up through the brush on game trails to the north or east ridges, then traverse into talus below the couloir. Otherwise, start up the Timpooneke Trail for 10 minutes, then work right up the ridge. Time: 2–3 hours.

The Climb: Ascend a pitch or two of 40-degree snow, some boulder moves, a few pitches of steeper snow, and a few more rock moves into the narrows where the slope angle reaches 55 degrees. Above this the route divides. Take the main couloir to the left. This can be a snow climb, mixed, or a scramble on rotten rock. At one point the ice steepens to 62 degrees. Near the end of the couloir, traverse up and right to ledges to the ridge. This is a hazardous climb. The debris on the snow and the dark runnel that runs down the couloir are stark rockfall warnings. Early morning starts will lessen the danger only slightly.

Descent: Descend the west ridge (2 hours, scrambling).

ASPEN GROVE AND SUNDANCE

The routes above Aspen Grove are best climbed early in the season, well before any significant snowfall. The avalanche danger is very significant later in the season.

6. TIMPANOGOS COULOIR (WI3–4, II)

Length: 600–700 feet.

Approach: From Provo Canyon, take Utah 92 (Alpine Loop Road) past Sundance to Aspen Grove (fee). Hike the Timpanogos Trail, past the first and second waterfalls, into the cirque above Aspen Grove. This is a couloir/gully high toward the right (northern) side of the cirque, in steppy cliffs where the trail past the final switchback crosses a large, steep drainage with a southeasterly aspect.

The Climb: Ascend directly up a steppy couloir. This climb is normally done in the fall. As winter progresses, the route becomes almost totally covered by snow, and only a few steep bulges remain uncovered.

Descent: Hike off to the south.

7. PICTURE WINDOW AND SKYLIGHT (WI3 AND WI4, I–II)

Length: 60 feet and 40 feet.

Approach: The routes are located high in the cirque and cannot be seen from the parking area. Take the Timpanogos Trail past the first and second waterfalls (good practice climbs), up the switchbacks into the cirque and past route 6. Watch for

Picture Window *and* Skylight. DOUG COATS PHOTO

Picture Window and *Skylight* about 3.5 miles from the trailhead, at the 9,000-foot level, near the central drainage. Time: 1.5 hours.

The Climb: *Picture Window:* Ascend a thin 30-foot curtain to lower-angled ice. *Skylight* is found in a large crack and chimney system in the rock band immediately above *Picture Window,* and it consists of a narrow chandelier through the back of the chimney.

Descent: From the top of *Skylight,* downclimb the snow slope to the right. At the top of *Picture Window,* rappel from small trees.

From the Timpanogos Trail several ice gullies can be seen dropping off the east face of Roberts Horn. These generally run between 3 to 5 pitches in length over very steppy terrain. The climbing is moderate, with occasional WI4 or 5 sections. Protection is difficult in some places, and climbers should plan on taking extra webbing and trash screws to leave behind on rappels.

Two steep 2-pitch routes reportedly have been done on the walls of Hidden Lake cirque. Hidden Lake can be reached along a marked trail which forks off from the Timpanogos Trail near the top of Primrose Cirque on its southern edge. The hike takes about two hours from Aspen Grove. The routes, known as *Moist and Juicy* and *Shower Curtain,* are both I4.

Primrose Cirque *and the cliffs below Roberts Horn.* Doug Coats photo

Stewart Falls. *Some interesting WI5 lines occasionally form on the rock faces to the left of the falls. The dagger to the right of the main falls is WI5–6.* BRIAN SMOOT PHOTO

8. STEWART FALLS (WI5, II)

Length: 220 feet.

Approach: This climb is located in the drainage below Big Provo and Cascade cirques (both cirques are indicated on USGS topos). There are two ways to approach it. The first is from the Sundance ski area (avoid the private housing area). From there, it's a 30 to 45-minute hike to the base of the falls. The other approach is via the Stewart Falls Trail from Aspen Grove. Time for this latter approach: at least 1 hour. Take avalanche precautions.

The Climb: Climb 2 pitches of steep ice. Belay midway at an alcove on the left.

Descent: Hike off to the right (north) and descend a gully.

MOUNT TIMPANOGOS, WEST SLOPE

9. PURE FUN (WI3–4, I)

Length: 75 feet.

Approach: From I-15, take exit 276 or 279 and follow the signs east to Pleasant Grove and into Battle Creek Canyon. Hike up the canyon 20 minutes from the Kiwana's Park. The route is found on the south slope on a north face.

The Climb: Short curtains and steps.

Descent: Rappel from trees.

Note: Other routes have been reported in Battle Creek Canyon, but most appear to be little more than boulder moves under 10m in length.

PROVO CANYON

Note on Parking: The two main parking areas for Routes 11 to 25 and Routes 34 to 36 are the View Area pullout and the Nunn's Park parking area. Both are signed. The View Area pullout is a paved area on the north side of US 189. Nunn's Park actually has two parking areas, one on each side of the highway (the Nunn's Park itself is on the north side). In winter it is usually only possible to access the parking area on the south side of the highway, so for the purposes of this book, all approaches are described from that parking area.

10. PIPEDREAM (WI3–4, I)

Length: 130–180 feet.

Approach: This route is located at the mouth of the canyon across from MM 8. Below the mouth of the canyon, just west of the junction of UT 52 and US 189, turn north along a service road (posted). Park and hike along the road to the base of some ice forming below a gigantic pipe.

The Climb: Climb any of several variations that merge about 50 feet up, after the crux moves. Follow thin ice over bulges and steps to the pipeline.

Descent: Rappel the route or follow the pipeline up-canyon and hike down.

11. FUDGEPACKER (WI5, I)

Length: Up to 90 feet.

Approach: This climb forms in the drainage just west of the large, arched strata folds. Park in the View Area pullout on the north side of the road at MM 10.5. Hike 30–40 minutes to the base of the climb, in the drainage to the west of the strata fold.

PROVO CANYON

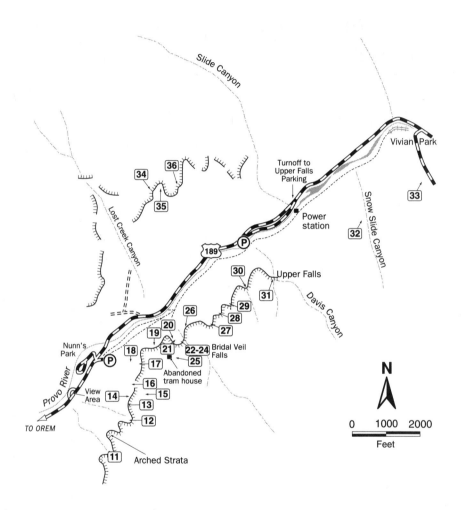

Fudgepacker (Route 11) can be seen to the right of the strata fold. The curtain below Fear of Motion *(Route 12) can be seen in the large drainage to the left of the fold.* DOUG COATS PHOTO

The Climb: 70 to 90 feet of very thin near-vertical ice that forms on either side of the waterfall.

Descent: Rappel from trees.

12. FEAR OF MOTION (WI4, II)

Length: Up to 540 feet.

Approach: From the View Area pullout, hike southeast into a large drainage east of the strata folds. Time: 30–40 minutes.

The Climb: Ascend an easy gully with bulges for 300 to 400 feet. The gully splits. Ascend the left fork for 80 feet to a 60-foot, near-vertical curtain. Note that much lower in the drainage the water from this climb forms another 30-foot vertical curtain over cliffs.

Descent: Rappel the crux and downclimb the gully.

13. ICEMATE (WI4, I)

Length: 50 feet.

Approach: About 200 yards east of the Route 12 drainage are two very obvious talus gullies. Take the west gully up to the cliffs. Time: 40 minutes from the View Area pullout or the Nunn's Park parking area.

The Climb: The route is located on the right side of the first cliff band. It consists of two near-vertical, 25-foot curtains.

Descent: Rappel from trees.

14. PLAYMATE (WI4, I)

Length: 60 feet.

Approach: As for Route 13.

The Climb: This route is found on the left side of the first cliff band. A 30-foot vertical curtain to a sloping edge and a steep 20-foot bulge.

Approach: Rappel from trees.

15. SOMETIMES (WI3, I)

Length: Up to 100 feet.

Approach: From the Nunn's Park parking area (MM 10.9), walk west a few minutes to a talus gully that leads up to cliffs. Time: 30 minutes.

The Climb: This is located a few hundred feet above Route 16. An easy gully that steepens to 85 degrees.

Descent: Rappel.

16. UNNAMED (WI2–3, I)

Length: Up to 215 feet.

Approach: This is located in a gully just right (west) of a large buttress. Approach from Nunn's Park.

The Climb: Flat-foot up gully ice for 80 feet and climb a moderate 15-foot bulge. Continue up low-angle snow or ice for 80 feet, then a thin moderate 30- to 40-foot bulge.

Descent: From the top of the first pitch traverse right and down. From the top of the second pitch rappel from small trees or downclimb and hike down right.

17. DAILY FEARS (WI4, I)

Length: 120 feet.

Approach: From the Nunn's Park parking lot, hike south up to the amphitheater cliff and either climb Route 18 or hike around it to the left or right. Continue hiking up the west side of the drainage about 10 minutes to the base of the climb.

The Climb: Ascend two 25-foot vertical curtains into an easy gully for 30 feet. Finish on a 15-foot curtain.

Descent: Rappel from trees on the right.

18. HELLO (WI4–5, I)

Length: Up to 80 feet.

Approach: Park at Nunn's Park and hike directly south into a large drainage to a wide cliff. 15 minutes.

The Climb: Ascend a thin, vertical curtain (40–60 feet) to low-angle ice.

Descent: Hike around the right (south) side.

19. STAIRWAY TO HEAVEN (WI5, III) ★★★

Length: Over 800 feet.

Approach: Park at Nunn's Park. Walk east 5 minutes, then hike up a talus-filled gully to the base of the climb; 25 minutes.

The Climb: The first pitch ascends two long tiers of a wide apron (WI3–5) to trees or bolts on a very wide ledge. The difficulty of this pitch varies with the start. On the left, the pitch is 200 feet and can be broken into two pitches for 50m ropes at a

Routes 17 and 18 are located in the drainage to the right of Stairway to Heaven *(far left profile). Nunn's Park is just out of the picture in the lower left corner.* DOUG COATS PHOTO

Stairway to Heaven. DAVE BLACK PHOTO

Doug Heinrich on the fifth pitch of Stairway to Heaven. CHRIS HARMSTON PHOTO

Bridal Veil and White Nightmare (right). Note the farmed routes on the right side of the second tier, high above the main falls. The long pillar is nearly 200 feet in length. DAVE BLACK PHOTO

midway ledge. Variations to the right are progressively shorter. The second pitch is half a rope length on an apron (WI4). Pitch 3: continue up a rope length on I4 flows to a belay/rappel station at a tree. Pitch 4: climb the short cone (WI3) to a wide ledge. Pitch 5: 100 feet of very steep ice to another wide ledge (WI5). Pitch 6: traverse left (east) along the ledge to the base of a 60-foot column (WI5). There are many bolts along the right margin of this climb. Belays can usually be set up on bolts at the back of the wide ledges or on runnered trees and boulders. Occasionally, two additional pitches come into shape. Pitch 7 is a narrow half-pitch column (WI6). The eighth pitch is another half-length of WI5.

Variations: There are dozens of minor and major variations of the standard route, including nearly two dozen mixed routes ranging from M4 to M9. Watch for the bolt ladders that protect many of these. *Prophet on a Stick* (WI6 or M7) seems to attract a lot of attention. It's a free hanging pillar about 80 feet to the left (east) of the WI3 cone of the 4th pitch. *Contrivance* (M8+) is a 5-bolt line to the hanging curtain left of the 5th pitch column. See Doug Heinrich's list of mixed picks in the introduction for basic information on additional mixed variations.

Descent: It's possible to rappel the route with two ropes. Stay on the right (west) margin to take advantage of the belay/rappel bolt stations and trees. From the top of the first pitch, it's possible to hike west along the ledge and around to the base. Along the ledges above the second, third, and fifth pitches, it's possible to hike or scramble eastward to the Bridal Veil drainage.

20. WHITE NIGHTMARE (WI4–5, I)

Length: 200 feet.

Approach: From Nunn's Park hike to the Bridal Veil area and up to the base of the dagger column on the far right side of the Bridal Veil amphitheater. 20 minutes.

The Climb: Ascend a 35-foot icicle and steep bulges that follow. The route can be done in a single lead (60m rope) to a set of rappel bolts or a runnered tree a few yards above them. Most often the route is done in two pitches, the first belayed at left-side bolts 80 feet from the base, and the second at bolts at 150 feet.

Descent: Descend by rappel from the tree or the bolts.

21. UNNAMED (WI5, I)

Length: 80 feet.

Approach: This climb often forms midway between Route 20 and Route 22. Approach as for Bridal Veil.

The Climb: A narrow pillar. Belay from bolts on the right of the top of the column.

Descent: Rappel from the same bolts.

22. BRIDAL VEIL RIGHT (WI4–5, I)

Length: 180 feet.

Approach: Approach as for Route 20. Time: 20 minutes. This is the right of two distinct flows of ice that form to the right of the main falls. (The main falls generally remain unfrozen all winter, but not always. See note below.)

The Climb: Climb a steep curtain and steppy bulges to the cliff rim.

Descent: Rappel from bolts or a tree. Alternatively, traverse east above the tops of the Bridal Veil routes, crossing the stream and working down into the amphitheater.

23. BRIDAL VEIL LEFT (WI4–5, I)

Length: 180 feet.

Approach: As for *White Nightmare* (Route 20) and *Bridal Veil Right* (Route 22).

Tim Stack leading a variation between the frozen main falls to his left and Route 23 to his right. BRIAN CABE PHOTO

The Climb: Climb a steep curtain or column, steppy bulges, and a steep finish.

Descent: As for *Bridal Veil Right* (Route 22).

24. UPPER BRIDAL VEIL (WI5, I–II)

Length: 180 feet.

Approach: Climb one of the lower Bridal Veil routes and traverse into the drainage to the base of the climb. Alternatively, hike up a trail just east of the main falls.

The Climb: Ascend a continuously vertical pillar or curain to a belay ledge (125 feet). Another short but steep pitch leads to the rim of the cliff. It's possible to do the entire route in a single lead using a 60m rope.

Descent: Traverse right (west) into the gully above routes 20–23. Rappel or downclimb (WI2–3) the gully and traverse east above the main falls to the trail.

Note: Contrary to popular belief, the main falls do freeze occasionally. At least two ascents have been made of the lower main falls. In the 1999-2000 season, some ice farming was done above Bridal Veil. Several routes briefly came to be, including a 200-foot pillar to the right of Upper Bridal Veil, visible in the photo of *Bridal Veil* and *White Nightmare*.

25. NOVA (WI3–4, II)

Length: 280 feet.

Approach: *Nova* is located on tiered cliffs to the left of the old tramway building, high in the Bridal Veil drainage. From the bottom of the amphitheater, either climb one of the *Bridal Veil* routes or hike up the descent route to gain the upper drainage and a moderate snow slope to the right. Ascend the snow slope to the base of the climb. Time: 1 hour from Nunn's Park.

The Climb: Ascend a series of 20- to 30-foot steps separated by wide ledges.

Descent: Rappel and downclimb the route.

26. ALL IS QUIET (WI5, I)

Length: 100 feet.

Approach: Hike east from Nunn's Park to the east side of the Bridal Veil amphitheater. Hike up the descent trail. This climb is a column near a giant tree just above the trail, after it turns west but before it crosses the stream. Time: 30 minutes from Nunn's Park.

The Climb: This is a 3-tiered column with some rock climbing to a ledge at the end.

Descent: Rappel from bolts along the ledge to the left (east).

27. FINGER OF FATE (WI4, II)

Length: 500 feet.

Approach: At MM 12.2, turn south and follow the road back west along the river for 0.4 mile. Park at the Upper Falls Picnic Area parking lot.

Brian Cabe on Finger of Fate. Melanie Mansfield PHOTO—Brian Cabe collection

Left to right: The Fang, Miller's Thriller, Post Nasal Drip, Finger of Fate. DAVE BLACK PHOTO

Cross the bridge and hike west a quarter mile. Hike up a gully to the base of the climb. Time: 35–40 minutes.

The Climb: Climb a steep, 130-foot corner and continue up short pillars or steps for three pitches.

Descent: Rappel the route. From the top of the first pitch, it's possible to scramble east along an exposed ledge to reach the bottom of the third pitch of Route 28 and the third pitch of Route 29.

28. POST NASAL DRIP (WI5, II) ★

Length: 400 feet.

Approach: Approach from the Upper Falls parking lot. This route is located east of Route 27. Time: 30–35 minutes.

The Climb: A moderate gully face leads up to a 65-foot column (pitches 1 and 2).

The third pitch is an 80-foot column followed by a final pitch over two shorter but steep bulges. *Snotty Nosed Brat* is *Post Nasal Drip* in lean conditions, when the upper columns haven't touched down and the route is M6 with some aid.

Descent: Rappel the route. The ledge at the base of the third pitch can be traversed east to *Miller's Thriller* or west to *Finger of Fate*.

29. MILLER'S THRILLER (WI3–4, II)

Length: 400 feet.

Approach: Approach from the Upper Falls parking lot. This route is in a gully east of Route 28. Time: 25–30 minutes.

The Climb: Ascend a wide WI3 gully (pitch 1) to a snow slope. Pitch 2 is a snow slope to the base of the crux face. Pitch 3 is a WI3–4 face to a tree. *Miller's Pillar* (WI5–6) is a third pitch variation that drops over an overhang to the left.

Descent: Rappel from the tree.

30. THE FANG (WI5, II) ★

Length: 400 feet.

Approach: From the Upper Falls parking area, hike 600 feet west and work up the drainage. *The Fang* is located east of Route 29. Time: 20–25 minutes.

The Climb: Two pitches up a wide WI3 apron and a laid-back snow gully lead to the base of a wonderful, delicate, 50-foot column known as "The Tube." This feature is the crux and final pitch.

Descent: Rappel from trees.

31. FMR WALL (WI4, I)

Length: 180 feet.

Approach: From the Upper Falls parking area, hike southeast into the major drainage east of Route 30 and hike up to the base. Time: 30–45 minutes. Otherwise, from the top of Route 30, traverse up and east into the drainage.

The Climb: A wide, 180-foot curtain.

Descent: Rappel from trees (two 60-meter ropes) or hike around.

32. EDGE OF SANITY (WI4, I–II)

Length: 210 feet.

Approach: From Vivian Park, hike 0.5 mile west around the ridge and down-canyon to Snow Slide Canyon. Hike up the canyon to a corner and dihedral system on the last major limestone buttress on the left

The Fang. BRIAN CABE PHOTO

(east). Time: 45–60 minutes. Notice the name of this canyon: it's an avalanche collector.

The Climb: Alternating short vertical curtains, ledges, steps, and narrow pillars. The crux pillar (30 feet) is on the final pitch. The route can be very thin and mixed. Carry a selection of rock gear.

Descent: Rappel off and hike down slopes to the right.

33. SOUTH FORK (WI3, I)

Length: 130 feet.

Approach: From Vivian Park, drive southeast along the South Fork road until you spot this route on the south slope.

The Climb: One pitch up a moderate chute.

Descent: Rappel or hike off.

Several routes are located in or near Lost Creek Canyon, on the north side of Provo Canyon. Lost Creek Canyon is the major drainage almost directly across from *Stairway to Heaven* (Route 19). There is much conflicting information about the names, lengths, and locations of these routes. The vague information that is available seems to place the route known as *Warm and Moist* on the cliffs in the main drainage of Lost Creek Canyon. Another route, *Forrest Gump*, apparently has been climbed on cliffs to the west of Lost Creek Canyon. Due to scanty and very conflicting information on both these climbs, neither is described in detail here.

34. AVALANCHE FALLS (WI4, I)

Length: 100 feet.

Approach: As for Route 35 (*Soft and Juicy*). This route is located just to the west of Route 35.

The Climb: A 35-foot curtain and a snow slope to a final 20-foot curtain.

Descent: Rappel from trees.

35. SOFT AND JUICY (WI5, II)

Length: 300 feet.

Lost Creek Canyon *as seen from* Stairway to Heaven. DAVE BLACK PHOTO

Soft and Juicy *(center) seen from* Stairway to Heaven. DAVE BLACK PHOTO

Approach: About 1,500 feet east of Lost Creek Canyon is a much smaller canyon, easily viewed from the highway. There are usually several pullouts available for parking. Thrash directly up to the canyon. 30–45 minutes.

The Climb: Ascend a few short pillars. A second pitch surmounts a 60-foot pillar and some shorter pillars above.

Descent: Rappel from trees or hike off.

36. SHOWER TOWER (WI5, I)

Length: 150 feet.

Approach: This route is located in a notch about 400 feet east of the mouth of the small canyon in which Route 35 (*Soft and Juicy*) is located.

The Climb: This is a two-tiered pillar (90 and 60 feet) with a small midway ledge.

Descent: Rappel or hike off.

ROCK CANYON

A number of routes have been done in Rock Canyon. Information is sketchy. Rock Canyon is located east of Provo. To reach it, drive north from downtown Provo or

The White Spider *ascends the gully behind the large pine on the right. Another flow can be seen behind the large cliff on the left.* DOUG COATS PHOTO

south from Provo Canyon on US 189. Drive east on 2230 North, then take 2300 North to Rock Canyon Park.

37. WHITE SPIDER (WI4, II)

Length: 130 feet.

Approach: Hike up Rock Canyon on the south slope to a major gully located about 0.5 mile from the locked green gate. Ascend the gully for a couple of thousand feet to the base of the climb. The gully is an avalanche collector. In 1967, a party of Boy Scouts was hit by a slide; one scout died under 12 feet of snow. Trees along the right side of the gully might provide some protection.

The Climb: A long pitch over steep, cauliflowered ice. The belay at the top is very difficult to protect.

Descent: Rappel from V-thread or bollards, or leave a screw.

Bill Bellcourt on Automatic Control Theory. CHRIS HARMSTON PHOTO

THE SOUTHERN WASATCH:

SANTAQUIN CANYON AND NORTH CREEK CANYON

Santaquin Canyon is located in the southern Wasatch Range, 20 miles south of Provo, out of the smog of Utah Valley and safe from the throngs of Provo Canyon climbers. It is one of the West's best concentrations of reliable, multipitch routes. Santaquin Canyon offers an exceptional variety of moderate to difficult fat climbs as well as a growing number of difficult mixed routes. The location is modestly remote but situated near the junctions of several major highways. It is definitely a worthwhile destination for out-of-state climbers and offers a nearby alternative to Provo and Maple Canyons. Contrary to popular rumor, the climbs in Santaquin Canyon are easy to locate and approach.

Climbing history: Although there was certainly some ice being done in the canyon by the early 1970s, the first recorded ascents of serious, multipitch routes came in 1978 when Doug Hansen and friends did *Squash Head* and *Backoff*. Mark Bennett and Brian Smoot climbed *Candlestick* and *Automatic Control Theory* in the early 1980s, and the team of Bennett, Smoot, and Robbins did the first ascent of *White Angel of Fear* in 1983. During the 1983–1984 season Jim Knight and Bruce Roghaar climbed *Frozen Assets* in North Creek Canyon. Doug Coats established several routes during the same period. Recently, difficult mixed routes have been put up by Doug Heinrich, Chris Harmston, Tim Wagner, Will Gadd, Robbie Coldert, and others.

Getting there: To find Santaquin Canyon from Interstate 15, take exit 248 (Santaquin) and drive south along a frontage road, then east into the canyon. Drive up the canyon as far as possible. The road is often in condition to drive as far as the Trumbolt picnic area. Ski or hike the remaining distance to Trumbolt as necessary. First-time visitors will want to get their bearings here. Standing at the bridge on the west end of the Trumbolt parking area, look east into the canyon and focus on the cliffs high on the south walls of the canyon. Framed in the 'V' of the canyon, one can see three major routes (assuming they are formed up): *The Candlestick* (Route 6), *Automatic Control Theory* (Route 8), and *Angel of Fear* (Route 9). Use these routes as points of reference.

SANTAQUIN CANYON AND NORTH CREEK CANYON

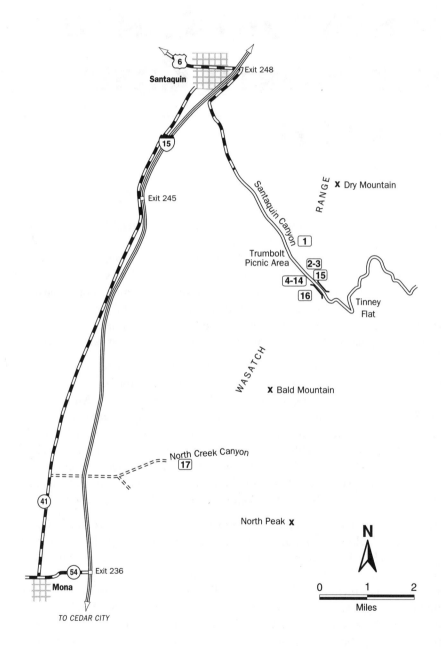

Bill Robbins on the first ascent of Angel of Fear *in 1983.* BRIAN SMOOT PHOTO

North Creek Canyon is found 10 miles south of Santaquin. From I-15, take exit 236 and drive a mile west on UT 54 to Mona. Turn north on Utah 41 and drive 2.2 miles. Take a right onto a dirt road and drive east under the interstate until you come to an obvious gravel pit operation. Continue on a rough road, trending northeast to the mouth of the canyon.

General Description: Santaquin Canyon has over 20 established routes and many variations. Lengths range from 60 to 500 feet. The climbing is at altitudes of from 6,000 to 7,800 feet on ice over limestone. Most routes were originally done using 50m ropes, but many of the rappels require double ropes. Helmets are recommended.

Climbing season: Good ice can usually be found from mid-December to late February or early March. Most of the routes are located on the south slope and are well protected from the sun.

Maps: Santaquin; Payson Lakes; Mona (for North Creek Canyon).

Other guidebooks: There is no guidebook to Santaquin Canyon ice. Check Tim Wagner's *Utah Ice* for updates.

Gear and guides: There are several climbing shops in the Provo area. See Appendix B for locations and telephone numbers. Check with Exum and the Provo shops for the availability of guides.

Camping and accommodations: Tinney Flat Campground is a 20-minute ski beyond the upper bridge. Climbers are often seen car-camping in the Trumbolt area parking lot, and so far nobody has reported getting hassled. With the proximity of hotels along the Wasatch Front, the possibilities are limitless. There is a group of inexpensive motels 15 miles south, off exit 225 in Nephi. There are plenty of motels to the north along the I-15 corridor.

Services: Gas and groceries are available in Nephi and Santaquin. Payson, Spanish Fork, and Provo are all within 30 minutes, and all have services.

Emergency services: Call 911 for all emergencies. Large hospitals are located in Payson and Provo, and there's a small hospital in Nephi. Air evac is available from Salt Lake City. Utah County has an excellent search and rescue team. Santaquin Canyon has its share of avalanches, and there have been several close calls on *Squash Head* in particular. Get an avalanche forecast (see Appendix C).

Nearby climbing and skiing: The ice in both Provo Canyon, to the north, and Maple Canyon, to the southeast, are easily within an hour's drive of Santaquin. Sundance Ski Area is located in Provo Canyon. The Wasatch Range is prime backcountry skiing territory.

SANTAQUIN CANYON

1. MR. FREEZE (WI4, II)

Length: 400 feet.

Approach: This route is located high on the north slope and requires an hour hike on steep slopes near the mouth of the canyon.

The Climb: The climb has a westerly aspect. Climb two 200-foot pitches up through a deep notch in the limestone cliffs. The notch fills with snow, and the climbing becomes easier as the season progresses.

Descent: Rappel from trees.

2. BOOZY THE CLOWN (WI5–6, I)

Length: 120–150 feet.

Approach: From the locked gate just above the bathrooms at the Trumbolt parking area, walk up the road into the canyon about 0.3 mile. When directly below *Automatic Control Theory* (Route 8), hike up the left (north) side of the canyon to the base of the route.

The Climb: This is a steep southwest-facing mixed route that rarely forms. Drytool (M6) to thin, steep ice on a face and follow it about 90 feet. The route is difficult to protect.

Descent: Rappel from a tree.

3. UNNAMED (WI3–4, II)

Length: 500 feet.

Approach: Hike up the north slope, directly across from *Automatic Control Theory* (Route 8).

The Climb: Follow a long gully over series of short steps and curtains.

Descent: Rappel from trees.

SANTAQUIN CANYON DETAIL

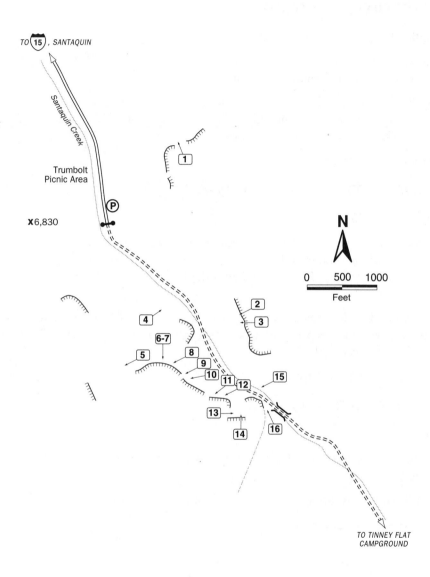

TO (15), SANTAQUIN

Santaquin Creek

Trumbolt
Picnic Area

X6,830

P

1

N

0   500   1000
Feet

2
3
4
6-7
5
8
9
10
11
12
15
13
14
16

TO TINNEY FLAT
CAMPGROUND

4. THE WATERFALL ROUTE (WI5, I)

Length: 100–150 feet.

Approach: This is located on the south slope below *Candlestick*. Where the road crosses the stream, go right and traverse to a major drainage. The route is located to the right (west) of the "Log Flume" sport-climbing wall. 10–15 minutes.

The Climb: Ascend an 80-foot pillar to easier ground and trees.

Descent: Rappel from trees.

5. MISTAKEN IDENTITY (WI4, I)

Length: 180 feet.

Approach: About 200 feet east of the locked gate, this route can be seen high on the south side, to the right of the major cliffs. To reach it, continue up the road from the locked gate 0.38 mile to where the stream switches from the south (right) side to the north side of the road. About 120 feet beyond this is a scree gully leading up to *The Candlestick* (Route 6). Ascend the gully, then go up around the right side of the major cliff, through the trees into the big drainage.

The Climb: Climb a moderately angled but steepening gully for 130 feet through a broken cliff band. Finish via a very steep, 30-foot wall.

Descent: A long, free-hanging rappel from trees on the left. It's also possible to traverse right for easier and shorter rappels from trees.

Tim Thompson on the first ascent of Mistaken Identity. Doug Coats photo

Left to right: White Angel of Fear, Automatic Control Theory, The Candlestick.
DON ROBERTS PHOTO

6. THE CANDLESTICK (WI5–6, I)

Length: 110 feet.

Approach: As described for the previous route, hike to a point 0.38 mile beyond the locked gate. High up on the right (south), the 3 routes that were visible from the lower bridge come into view. The approach gully is another 120 feet beyond.

The Climb: This is a steep, slightly stepped pillar.

Descent: Rappel.

7. SWOLLEN CHEEK (M7–8 OR WI4 IF COMPLETELY FORMED, II)

Length: 210 feet.

Approach: Approach as for Route 6.

The Climb: This ascends the rock face just under the right margin of Route 8. Climb past 4 bolts and continue along the right margin of the ice past 2 more bolts to the top.

Descent: Rappel as for Route 8.

The Candlestick.

Chris Harmston leading Swollen Cheek.

8. AUTOMATIC CONTROL THEORY (WI5–6, II) ★★

Length: 210 feet.

Approach: Approach as for Route 6.

The Climb: A steep WI4 pitch (100 feet) followed by a 110-foot WI5 pillar. This route is consistently difficult. It's possible to skirt the first pitch by climbing M6 from the right (4 bolts).

Descent: Rappel from trees.

9. WHITE ANGEL OF FEAR (WI5–6, II) ★★

Length: 210 feet.

Approach: Leave the road about 0.41 mile above the gate and follow a gully to the base.

The Climb: A beautiful pillar, which rarely forms completely. Climb a steep curtain to a snow ledge at the base of the pillar. Climb the pillar directly, belaying midway (the first ascent party belayed from an ice cave). Several variations have been completed. *Lu-*

Automatic Control Theory. BRIAN CABE PHOTO

cifer (M8 ★) is described as seven bolts that lead up and behind the bottom dagger and end at a 2-bolt belay. A variation called *M7* (named after its M7 rating) ascends an arch to a bolt to the left of the bottom dagger. From there, it moves right and onto the dagger. Heinrich has noted a variation to the right of the top of the ice, called *Dark Angel* (M9).

Descent: Rappel from trees and bolts (2 two-rope rappels).

10. RICOCHET (WI6–7, M6–7, AO II) ★

Length: 250 feet.

Approach: From the ledge atop the ice curtain below *Angel of Fear*, traverse left about 50 feet.

The Climb: Follow thin and mixed past 4 bolts to a 2-bolt belay on the left, below a short ice dagger. Climb the dagger on the right (bolt), then move up left and ascend

(A0 or possibly M9) past 3 bolts to the final delicate climb along the left side of a long pillar.

Descent: Rappel from a tree on the left, then bolts (two 2-rope 60m rappels).

11. SQUASH HEAD, A.K.A. SQUASH HEAD NOSE (WI3–4, I)

Length: 300 feet.

Approach: This route is located on the south slope, close to the road, 0.51 mile beyond the locked gate, 0.1 mile past the Route 6 approach gully).

The Climb: A 35-foot, near-vertical curtain leads to a 240-foot gully. The lower pitch can be avoided via rock to the east. A route called *Martini* is a mixed line of 10 bolts (A0, M8–9) starting about 15 feet to the left of the base of the climb. It can be used (aided) to gain the gully when the vertical curtain is gone.

Descent: Rappel the route, or at the top of the route, climb a short section on the east (left) side and drop into the next canyon to the base of *Backoff* (Route 13).

Ricochet (10) *left*, White Angel of Fear (9) *right*.
CHRIS HARMSTON PHOTO

Chris Harmston on Ricochet (10).
DOUG HEINRICH PHOTO

Squash Head. DON ROBERTS PHOTO

12. BETTER THAN BAGHDAD (M7–9, I)

Length: 70 feet.

Approach: Located in a cave a few minutes from the road and 300 feet east from the base of *Squash Head* (Route 11).

The Climb: Climb a mixed line on the left and traverse onto the WI4 pillar. There are other mixed lines being established as this is being written.

Descent: Rappel from bolts a few yards beyond the lip of the roof.

13. BACKOFF (WI4–5, I) ★★

Length: 165–200 feet.

Approach: From the top of *Squash Head* (Route 11), climb a short section of rock, then rappel east into the next canyon. From the road, at 0.53 miles beyond the locked gate, hike directly up the gully beneath the climb.

The Climb: Climb a moderate, full pitch of 50-degree ice, and another shorter pitch of 70–80 degrees. The

Squash Head *(right)*, Better than Baghdad *(hidden behind trees, lower left corner)*, Backoff *(in the drainage above and just left of* Squash Head*)*, *and* Get Back On It *(left)*.
DAVE BLACK PHOTO

actual length of the first pitch varies with the amount of snow covering it.

Descent: Double-rope rappel from a tree just east of the climb.

14. GET BACK ON IT (WI4, I)

Length: 100 feet.

Approach: This route is located 200 feet east of *Backoff* (Route 13).

The Climb: Very thin ice over a face. There may be some old bolts still in place.

Descent: Rappel and hike down the *Backoff* gully.

15. UNNAMED (WI3, I)

Length: Many variations up to 500 feet.

Bruce Bidner on Backoff. BRIAN CABE PHOTO

Approach: Hike 250 feet east along the road beyond the *Backoff* gully and look north across the stream to view the route(s). Crossing the stream here can be an unpleasant slog in deep snow. Another option is to cross at the upper bridge, then work back west.

The Climb: This is a wide gully with many variations. The ice is usually thin.

Descent: Rappel from trees along most variations.

16. CRYSTAL CIRCUMSTANCE, A.K.A. BRIDGE GULLY (WI2, I)

Length: 60–200 feet.

Approach: Hike east to just below the upper bridge, which is located 430 feet from the gully to *Backoff*. Just before the bridge, turn south into a gully.

The Climb: Start at the bridge and ascend various bulges and gullies. There are many variations.

Descent: Hike down the gully.

Get Back On It *(left) and* Backoff. DON ROBERTS PHOTO

Note: A short route consisting of four bolts to a hanging curtain called *Baby Bitch* (M8, I) is located 10 minutes beyond the upper bridge to the north of the road.

NORTH CREEK CANYON

17. FROZEN ASSETS (WI4, II–III)

Length: 1,000 feet.

Approach: From the mouth of the canyon, approach along the streambed to the gully below the climb. Time: 60 minutes to the base. The climb is on the south slope and faces northwest.

The Climb: *Frozen Assets* has a steep start (70 degrees) and runs up to 8 pitches over a web of aprons and bulges, generally WI3 with some short WI4 sections. The first ascent party of four split into two teams and took different lines. Recon with a good set of binoculars from the highway before committing to the approach.

Descent: Rappel from trees. Double 60m ropes will make the descent easier and safer.

THE BASIN AND RANGE PROVINCE

Basically, this area is west of Interstate 15 and north of the Pine Valley Mountains. It has not seen much in the way of ice climbing. The potential is there, but likely areas are very remote, and the road system can be problematic in the winter. Still, some short ice climbs have been done in Granite and Red Cedar Canyons on the east slope of the Deep Creek Range. A handful of Salt Lake City climbers have endured long approaches to climb routes in the east slope cirques of the Stansbury Mountains, and exploration of some transient lines of ice has taken place near Fish Springs and Notch Peak. On the edge of the Sevier Desert, along the east slope of the Canyon Mountains north of Holden, a half-dozen steep, multipitch lines have been observed in the cliffs just below the summit of 9,236-foot Williams Peak. Undoubtedly, there are many similar possibilities in the small mountain ranges of the region.

Ice on Stansbury Peak. BRIAN CABE PHOTO

THE BASIN AND RANGE PROVINCE

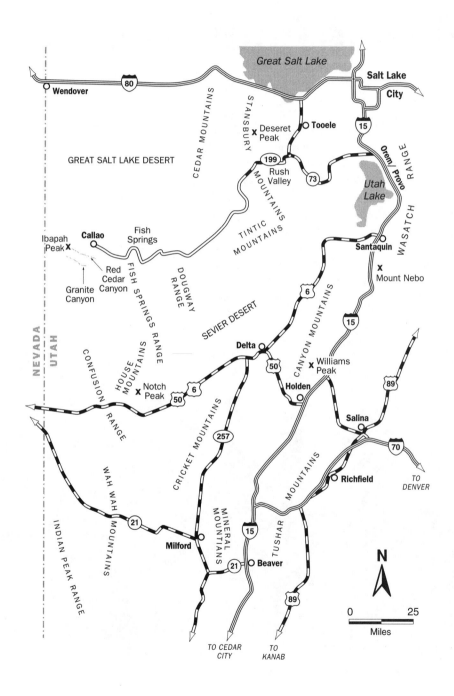

Great Salt Lake

Salt Lake City

Wendover

80

GREAT SALT LAKE DESERT

CEDAR MOUNTAINS

STANSBURY MOUNTAINS

✗ Deseret Peak

Tooele

15

199

Rush Valley

73

Orem/Provo

Utah Lake

WASATCH RANGE

Fish Springs

TINTIC MOUNTAINS

Santaquin

Ibapah Peak ✗

Callao

✗ Mount Nebo

Red Cedar Canyon

FISH SPRINGS RANGE

DOUGWAY RANGE

6

Granite Canyon

SEVIER DESERT

CANYON MOUNTAINS

Delta

15

NEVADA

UTAH

CONFUSION RANGE

HOUSE MOUNTAINS

✗ Notch Peak

50

6

50

Williams Peak ✗

Holden

89

Salina

70

257

CRICKET MOUNTAINS

Richfield

TO DENVER

WAH WAH MOUNTAINS

21

MINERAL MOUNTAINS

15

TUSHAR MOUNTAINS

N

INDIAN PEAK RANGE

Milford

21

Beaver

89

0   25

Miles

TO CEDAR CITY

TO KANAB

With the exception of Milford and areas immediately adjacent to U.S. Highway 6/50, I-80, and I-15, there are few services in the west desert. Once you leave the main highway, there is virtually nowhere to purchase food or fuel, and emergency services are difficult to obtain. Go prepared.

Doug Coats on the first ascent of Billies Icicle. ALAN MCQUIVEY PHOTO—DOUG COATS COLLECTION

EASTERN UTAH

For purposes of this book, "Eastern Utah" is the area north of Interstate 70, east of Utah 10, and east of the Wasatch Mountains. This is very mountainous and rugged country. The Uinta Mountains contain the highest summits in the state, and there's plenty of ice to be done. Aerial photographs of many of the cirques in winter reveal clusters of water ice. In the summer, a small number of short alpine ice climbs exist for those who are willing to hike the miles required to reach them. Plenty of short routes have been done in Indian, Price, and Spanish Fork Canyons. But where are the rumored megaroutes of eastern Utah? Like those of Zion National Park, nobody really seems to have done them or can even say with any authority where they might be. One reliable source claims to have found a canyon "between Vernal and the Uintas that puts Provo Canyon to shame." Guidebooks are information catalysts: undoubtedly information will come to light after this book is published.

Climbing history: Doug Coats figured prominently in the climbs of Spanish Fork, Diamond Fork, and Indian Canyon in the 1980s. Jerry Cole, Dave Black, and other Ogden climbers did much of the ice in Echo Canyon in 1982–1983. The lack of data prevents a more extensive and detailed history of ice climbing in the area.

Getting there: The Spanish Fork Canyon and Price Canyon climbs can all be accessed along U.S. Highway 6. The Diamond Fork routes can be reached from US 6 on the Diamond Fork Canyon Road near Thistle.

Indian Canyon lies along US 191, and the Uinta Mountains routes are generally accessed from US 191/40 from the east and south, UT 150 from the west, and the North Slope Road and trailhead roads south of I-80 from the north.

The northern San Rafael Swell is most easily reached from UT 10 along the Green River Cutoff Road and Buckhorn Wash Road east of Castle Dale. See Route 21 for more details on the drive.

Echo Canyon can be accessed from Ogden via I-84, and from Salt Lake City and Evanston via I-80.

General Description: Most of the routes described here are short and form over sandstone at relatively low altitudes (5,000 to 7,500 feet). The notable exceptions are routes in the Uinta Mountains, which form at altitudes up to 13,000 feet or higher over metamorphic rocks of various types, primarily quartzite.

A reminder to the reader: only climbs over 10m in length (33 feet) are described in this guide book. There are dozens of small ice flows in Diamond Fork, Price, Spanish Fork, and Indian Canyons that do not meet that requirement.

EASTERN UTAH

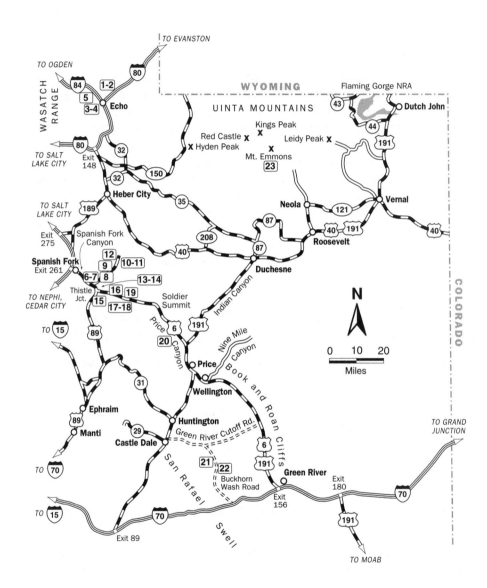

Climbing season: The lower altitude routes are fickle and melt out frequently. Ice in the upper altitudes of the Uinta Mountains either stays all year ("alpine ice") or forms early. Substantial water ice lines have been noted on north face cliffs as early as late September.

Ethics and access: Most of the eastern Utah routes are located on public lands. In some cases it may be necessary to cross mining property, ranches, and the Uintah and Ouray Indian Reservation. The author is unaware of major access issues. In the past there have some problems accessing certain areas of the southern slope of the Uinta Mountains through the reservation. Climbers should obtain permission where necessary.

Maps: Buck Knoll (Indian Canyon); Jones Hollow (Indian Canyon); Billies Mountain (Diamond Fork); Thistle (Spanish Fork Canyon); Mill Fork (Spanish Fork); Kyune (Price Canyon); Mt. Emmons; Bob Hill Knoll (Mt. Emmons).

Other guidebooks: There are no ice climbing or comprehensive rock climbing guidebooks for eastern Utah. Stewart Green's *Rock Climbing Utah* contains a good selection of rock routes in the San Rafael Swell, and there are several excellent hiking guides to the Uinta Mountains and the San Rafael Swell. The best sources for those are the larger book shops on the Wasatch Front.

Gear and guides: It's probably safe to say that there are no resident experts on eastern Utah ice. However, there is no lack of non-climbing guide services and outfitters.

Camping and accommodations: There are hundreds of public campgrounds in the Ashley and Uintah National Forests. Car camping in remote areas is normally not a problem. Hotels are available in Vernal, Roosevelt, Duschene, Price, Spanish Fork, Heber City, Ogden, Salt Lake City, Evanston, and Green River (Wyoming).

Services: Gas, groceries, banking, and restaurant services are available in the same towns (above).

Emergency services: Call 911 for all emergencies. There are hospitals in Vernal, Roosevelt, Price, Heber City, Ogden, Salt Lake City, and Evanston. Air evac is available from the Wasatch Front. Get an avalanche forecast and an extended weather forecast before going into the Uinta Mountains (see Appendix C).

Nearby climbing and skiing: The towns of eastern Utah are quite removed from the major ice climbing and commercial ski areas of the state. Sundance, Deer Valley, and Park City are the logical ski destinations if one simply can't do without groomed runs.

ECHO CANYON

The red sandstone narrows of Echo Canyon are located about 45 minutes east of both Ogden and Salt Lake City, nestled between the Bear River, Wasatch Range, and Uinta Mountains. Numerous flows form here from time to time. Most of them are short pillars and gullies 30 to 60 feet in length. Some can be linked to contrive interesting routes.

1. DREAMBOAT ANNIE (WI4–5, I)

Length: 200 feet.

Approach: From exit 169 off I-80, drive along the frontage road on the north until 0.3 mile past a road maintenance station. Hike a few hundred yards up the large side canyon. The climb is located on the east side. Time: 20 minutes.

The Climb: Ascend four vertical steps of from 30 to 60 feet each, separated by wide, low-angle ledges. The climb ends on the rim of the canyon.

Descent: Rappel from trees.

2. PENCIL PILLAR (WI5–6, I)

Length: 125 feet.

Approach: Continue up the same side canyon. This is located a few hundred feet north of Route 1.

The Climb: This amazing, thin pillar is a straight shot off the overhanging rim.

Descent: Double-rope rappel from trees.

3. SHAKE 'EM KRIS AND PERT LI'L HUMMERS (WI2–3, I)

Length: 100 feet each.

Approach: These two routes are in the left of two shallow bowls on the redrock cliffs on the hillside south of Echo, just west of and visible from the junction of I-80 and I-84. Take one of the Echo exits and drive south from Echo on the Bromley Canyon road. Park by the hill and hike 20 minutes to the cliffs.

The Climbs: These are two slabby lines that converge near the base. *Shake 'Em* is on the left.

Descent: Rappel the route.

4. NAKED IN TENNIES (WI4, I)

Length: 130 feet.

Approach: As for Route 3. This climb is located in the right bowl.

The Climb: Climb a short curtain to a narrow ledge and continue up a steep, 40-foot face. Steppy ice leads to a low-angle gully.

Descent: Rappel from a tree.

5. THE LEFT AND RIGHT SCREAMERS (WI4, I)

Length: 80–100 feet.

Approach: Both climbs are located above MM 111.8, just above I-84 on the south side. Park as close as possible, wherever it's convenient and legal (this will require some creativity). Climbers commonly park their vehicles in the emergency lane and jump the barrier. This is a dangerous and illegal practice.

The Climbs: These are 2 parallel flows on the broken, roadside face. The climbs go directly up the thin ice. Both are very difficult to protect.

Descent: Rappel from boulders or small trees.

Note: From the top of the *Screamers* a short hike to the right (west) along the ledge leads to an 80-foot, WI3 smear in an alcove.

DIAMOND FORK CANYON

6. SPECTATOR FALLS (WI4–5, I)

Length: 70 feet.

Approach: From a junction with US 6 about 2 miles northwest of the Thistle Slide overlook, drive about 2 miles up the Diamond Fork Canyon Road. Watch for a livestock corral on the left. This route is located on a small, yellow sandstone crag on the left (north) side of the canyon. Hike a few minutes to the base.

The Climb: Ascend 15 feet of moderate ice to a ledge and a 40-foot vertical wall.

Descent: Hike off to the left (west).

7. WHITE ON RED (WI4, I)

Length: 90 feet.

Approach: In the red cliffs, about 7.5 miles up the Diamond Fork road, look on the left (north) side of the canyon below an obvious thumb of rock. Scramble to the base.

The Climb: Thirty feet of thin, moderate ice to a thin, near-vertical 40-foot step. A short hike up the gully leads to another vertical step (17 feet).

Descent: Downclimb via ledges to the left.

DIAMOND FORK DETAIL

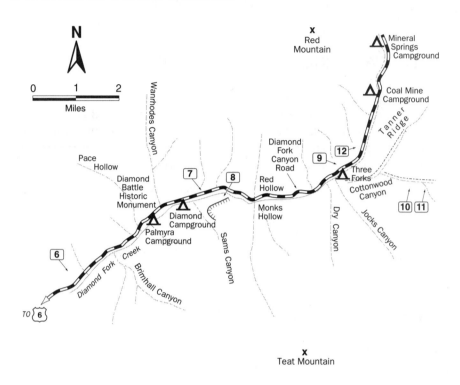

8. SILVER STREAM (WI3–4, I)

Length: 300–400 feet.

Approach: About 8 miles up the Diamond Fork road in the red cliffs area, there's a large sandstone buttress on the right (east) side. The route forms in the deepest of several smooth gullies on the hillside immediately up-canyon from the buttress. Cross the stream and hike to the base.

The Climb: Follow thin and difficult-to-protect ice at a moderate angle to the ridge.

Descent: Scramble and hike to either side.

9. CONGLOMERATE FALLS (WI3–4, I)

Length: 50 feet.

Approach: Up the Diamond Fork road, 10.5 miles from the US 6 junction, and immediately before the Three Forks turnout, is a gully that splits conglomerate crags that come near the edge of the road. A brief hike leads up the gully to the climb.

The Climb: Steps and bulges for 50 feet.

Descent: Traverse left beyond the cliff and hike down the slope and back into the gully.

10. TOADSTOOL ICE WALL (WI5, I)

Length: 250 feet.

Approach: Park at the Three Forks turnout and hike up the hot springs trail (right fork) for 0.75 mile. Watch for a large boulder that looks like a toadstool off the side of the trail. From there, hike across the creek and to the base of the climb. Time: 30 minutes.

The Climb: Scramble up a snow slope to a 20-foot step. Continue on snow for 60 feet to ice on the left side of the cliff. Ascend a 20-foot column and 100 feet of steep and steppy ice. Traverse a ledge right to the final 50-foot ice wall.

Descent: Rappel the route.

11. SIXTH WATER (WI3–4, I)

Length: 100 feet.

Approach: Continue another 0.25 mile up the hot springs trail. Cross the stream and get on the ice.

The Climb: Short steps and bulges.

Descent: Rappel.

12. BARELY THERE (WI5, I)

Length: 40 feet.

Approach: This short route is located behind some trees along a left (west) side crag about 0.6 mile past the Three Forks turnout.

The Climb: Ascend a thin, 20-foot curtain, hike briefly, then climb a steep 20-foot sliver (mixed).

Descent: Rappel or scramble around the crag.

SPANISH FORK AND PRICE CANYONS

13. BILLIES ICICLE (WI4–5, I)

Length: 120 feet.

Approach: This is located on the east side of US 6 near the pass, about 1.5 miles south of the junction with Diamond Fork Canyon Road and 0.6 mile north of the

Doug Coats on the first ascent of Conglomerate Falls. DOUG COATS COLLECTION

Thistle Slide overlook. There is a dirt parking area directly below the climb. Bushwhack up the left side of the gully until it's possible to drop into it and reach the base of the route; 10 minutes.

The Climb: This route faces west and is often thin and hollow. Follow moderate ice for 60 feet and surmount a 20-foot vertical section. Continue on lower angle ice to the finish.

Descent: Rappel the route.

14. IRON OXIDE FALLS (WI3–4, I)

Length: 90 feet.

Approach: On the east side of the road, 0.4 mile south of *Billies Icicle*. Hike up and drop into the gully from the left. Scramble up the gully to the base of the ice. Time: 10 minutes.

The Climb: Thirty feet of near-vertical ice through a tight notch/chimney followed by 60 feet of steep ice above and to the right.

Descent: Traverse left past the cliff band and scramble down the slope north of the climb.

15. WILD BULL (WI5, I)

Length: 70 feet.

Approach: From the abandoned town of Thistle, drive (4WD) or ski 2.3 miles up Lake Fork Canyon. Park across from a ranch. The climb is across the field to the east.

The Climb: A narrow, vertical, chandeliered and cauliflowered column.

Descent: Hike the road to the left of the route.

16. CHIP-N-EASY (WI3–4, I)

Length: 50 feet.

Approach: On the north side of US 6, about 3 miles east of the pass (Thistle Slide) are some livestock corrals. Park nearby and hike a quarter mile up a small box canyon to the left; 10 minutes.

The Climb: Climb a narrow, 25-foot near-vertical step and a narrow, 15-foot vertical column. Scramble briefly and climb a final 10-foot vertical step.

Descent: Scramble down along either side of the climb.

17. THE LEAST COMPLICATED, A.K.A. TLC (WI4–5, I)

Length: 110 feet.

Approach: This route is located in a narrow slot canyon across from a big cave at MM 191.2 on US 6, at the beginning of the Red Narrows. Cross the stream and climb a snow slope down-canyon from the slot. Follow a ridge up and left until it's possible to traverse to the top of the slot. Rappel to the base from trees. One hour. Alternatively, hike to the bottom of the slot and make difficult free moves or aid (bolts) into the slot below the climb.

The Climb: Twenty feet of vertical and overhanging ice followed by 90 feet at 70 to 80 degrees.

Descent: Hike down the approach from the top of the climb, or from inside the slot, downclimb and rappel from trees to the base of the gully.

18. QUESTION MARK (WI5–6, I)

Length: 120 feet.

Approach: Approach as for Route 17. This route is in the same slot on the opposite wall.

The Climb: Thin and questionable. Stem between the two routes until there's enough ice to swing onto, or do thin mixed climbing up a slab or an overhang. Continue up 30 feet of vertical and steppy ice. The angle eases from there.

Descent: Descend as from Route 17.

19. THE GREAT GULLY CLIMB (WI4, I)

Length: 400 feet.

Approach: Located 0.5 mile east of the cave (Route 17), in redrock crags on the north side of US 6.

The Climb: Scramble up the gully. Ascend 35 feet of steppy, vertical ice. Scramble farther up the gully, keeping to the right, to a series of 20-foot walls and columns interspersed with long stretches of broken gully ice and mixed climbing.

Descent: Scramble around the rock bands and ice to the base.

20. TINKERTOYS, A.K.A. DIRTCICLE, PRICECICLE (WI4, I)

Length: 60 feet.

Approach: In a deep cleft right off the west side of the road at MM 223.6.

The Climb: Steep ice to a rim. A similar (twin) flow has been climbed on the left side of this alcove.

Descent: Rappel the route or hike around to the right (north).

INDIAN CANYON

Indian Canyon is located in the Ashley National Forest along the north slope of the West Tavaputs Plateau between the towns of Price and Duschesne on US 191. This canyon is frequently confused with Indian Creek, the southern Utah crack-climbing mecca to which it bears absolutely no resemblance. During research for this book, it was necessary for the author to decipher conflicting 15-year-old notes from two different climbers. From the data available, it can be surmised they did about 15 routes. Since their mile marker notations did not coincide, several near-fruitless field trips were made to the area to try to pinpoint the locations of those routes. Note that these routes form over a few bands of shale cliffs varying from 20 to 40 feet thick. Longer cruxes form where the cliffs are undercut, but most of the routes are either very short "boulder" problems or a series of "boulder" problems separated by large ledges or gullies. All are within a 20-minute hike of the road. The author found ice in side canyons and roadside notches at the following locations in the Left Fork of Indian Canyon along US 191:

MM 175.8, west side: 50-foot curtain.

MM 175.9, west side: Shaley cliff band 200 feet wide, with several 15- to 30-foot curtains.

MM 176.15, west side: Several 20- to 30-foot curtains.

MM 176.4, west side: In the right fork of a side canyon, 20- to 30-foot curtains.

MM 177.8, west side: 40-foot curtain.

MM 178, east side: Indian Canyon Guard Station.

MM 178.2, west side: 30-foot curtains on the north slope of Grass Hollow Canyon.

MM 178.4, west side: 20- to 30-foot curtains on the north slope of a side canyon.

MM 178.6, west side: 20- to 30-foot curtains close to the road.

MM 178.65, east side: Fat, 20-foot curtain.

MM 180.9, west side: A series of 20-foot steps into a low-angle gully, another 20-foot curtain and a 40-foot cone/column; 170 feet total (possibly Doug Coats's *Rotten Eggs* route).

MM 182.9, west side: 20-foot dagger.

MM 185, west side: 40-foot curtain in a narrow canyon behind the forest boundary sign.

MM 186.3, west side: 30- to 40-foot curtain through a notch to a gully and a 10-foot dagger.

MM 187.3, west side: Several small bulges along the streambed 20 minutes up the side canyon.

Tim Thompson on Rotten Eggs. DOUG COATS PHOTO

MM 187.8, east side: 70 feet on stepped columns to a gully and a final 30-foot column.

MM 190.3, east side: Steep, tiered 50-foot curtain and a 20-foot column.

MM 192.8, east side: 80 feet of enjoyable but thin WI4 in a deep alcove cleft; approach along the right side and drop into the drainage.

MM 194, east side: Short curtains.

Descents from most of these short climbs can be accomplished by hiking briefly to adjacent slopes, where the cliff thins out or disappears. Most could also be easily rappelled.

Rumor has it that the best ice in the area is not in the Left Fork but the Right Fork of Indian Canyon. Unfortunately the access to the Right Fork is private and the author found the gate (MM 191) locked and guarded by a large and very assertive dog.

THE SAN RAFAEL SWELL AND THE BOOK AND ROAN CLIFFS

The San Rafael Swell has some serious potential for tough ice routes. Unfortunately, the area lies in the rain shadow of the Wasatch Plateau and likely drainages are at relatively low altitudes. Anyone finding ice here will have to be in the right place at the right time. In the early 1990s, the author made several early- to mid-January exploratory trips into the Swell and the Book and Roan Cliffs. During one particularly cold season, some short pillars and curtains were found in Nine Mile Canyon, and two minor routes were done along the Buckhorn Wash in the Swell (below). As in Zion, Capitol Reef, Escalante, and Moab, the best chance for reliable routes probably lies deep in the slots.

21. SAN RAFAEL SMELL (WI4–5, I)

Length: 150 feet.

Approach: From Utah 10 just north of Castle Dale, take the Green River Cutoff Road (poorly marked) east 14.5 miles to a junction and turn right (southerly) into Buckhorn Wash. Follow Buckhorn Wash Road 3.3 miles and park at a large pullout about a half-mile south of Little Holes Canyon. This canyon is marked on the USGS topo, but not in DeLorme's *Utah Atlas*. The best reference is Steve Allen's book *Canyoneering: The San Rafael Swell* (see Appendix A). Route 21 is located in the back of a small, narrow canyon to the west. Hike about 2,000 feet to the base of the climb.

The Climb: A curtain over the canyon rim.

Descent: Rappel from trees.

22. FOOL'S COLD (WI5, I)

Length: 300 feet.

Approach: Follow approach information for Route 21 to the pullout. From there, continue south along Buckhorn Wash Road another 5.1 miles. Route 22 is found east of the road, 1.5 miles north of the Buckhorn Wash Bridge, in a gully on the northwest slope of a mountainous crag called April Fool's Buttress. The gully is referred to as Fool's Canyon by rock climbers. Time: 30 minutes to get into the gully and up to the ice.

The Climb: Steppy gully ice over some short curtains and a couple of narrow, 30-foot columns.

Descent: Scramble and rappel the route.

THE UINTA MOUNTAINS

There's probably enough winter ice in the Uinta Mountains for a book of its own. Some insignificant falls have been done in the drainages northeast and northwest of Red Castle Peak and there have been impressive slivers of winter ice sighted on its cliffs. This is probably representative of many of the peaks. The problem is not a lack of ice, it's the horrendous approaches required to access the high peaks and remote canyons of the range.

One would expect more alpine ice than is present in this line of 13,000-foot peaks lying east of a large body of water (The Great Salt Lake). Unfortunately, the selection of alpine ice routes is very limited.

23. MOUNT EMMONS, NORTH FACE COULOIR (AI2–3, III–IV)

Length: 1,200 feet.

Approach: This face is best approached from the Uinta River Canyon (U-Bar Ranch). This 30-mile round trip has been done solo in a very long day, but climbers should plan on a minimum of two full days. A few miles up the trail, take the left fork and cross the river on a large, steel bridge. Follow the trail through the Chain Lakes Basin to Robert's Pass. Continue along a trail from the pass past B-29 and Carrot Lakes and around a ridge into the north face cirque. From the permanent snowfield, work up the central gully to the couloir.

The Climb: Follow the couloir directly up through a deep notch in a big cliff band until it ends in a steep, broken headwall several hundred feet under the summit. An exposed scramble to the right leads to a slightly corniced snowfield. This traverse is probably easier along a couple of right-side ramps lower in the couloir. The couloir averages just under 40 degrees and reaches over 50 degrees in several places.

Descent: Descend a long, rocky northeast ridge and work into either Robert's Pass or the upper Chain Lakes basins just south of the pass.

Note: In the fall, before heavy snows become a problem, many climbers visit the cirques on the north side of Leidy Peak. Several flows are reported to form there. Access the area via Red Cloud Loop/Dry Fork Loop road either through Dry Fork Canyon northeast of Vernal or from US 191 midway between Vernal and Flaming Gorge. Follow the signs to Trout Creek Park and Hacking Lake. There are several cirques in the vicinity.

FLAMING GORGE

Either there isn't much climbing to be done in the vicinity of Flaming Gorge, or climbers just aren't talking about it. To the west of the spillway, there's a low-angle, 200-foot flow that occasionally gets climbed. Most of the climbers who are interested in the area are convinced that the real climbs lie downstream, probably off the cliffs along the south shore of the river.

Seth Shaw on Get Whacked. DOUG HEINRICH PHOTO

THE SAN PITCH MOUNTAINS: MAPLE CANYON

When you ask climbers about Maple Canyon you get a wide range of opinions. Maple Canyon's ice is steep, challenging, and thin. It's also unreliable. One year the routes may be fat and numerous, the next year they might be nonexistent. A few hours of sunshine or an afternoon rain can wipe the walls clean of ice. Yet when the ice is "in" there may be hundreds of prime routes to pick from. The canyon is frequently compared to the ice park in Ouray, Colorado, but Ouray would come in a distant second place to Maple Canyon on a good Maple day. In this chapter of *Ice Climbing Utah,* 33 of the most popular or highly recommended Maple Canyon routes are included. For comprehensive coverage of the area, purchase Jason Stevens's upcoming guidebook (see below).

Climbing history: The earliest known routes in Maple were moderate climbs by today's standards, put up by Toni Valdez, Virgil Ash, and Matt and Paul Frank from 1982 to 1984. The information on their routes in the main canyon and "The Corridor" (Box Canyon) is sketchy. In 1987–1988 the author climbed several new routes.

The last half of the 1990s saw tremendous development and an enormous influx of climbers. First ascensionists during that period included Doug Heinrich, Steve House, Robbie Colbert, Jason Stevens, Tim Wagner, Todd Murray, Chris Harmston, Seth Shaw, Bob Swenson, Keith Royster, Bill Ohran, Jared Nielson, Brian Cabe, Boone Speed, and Zach Bishop. The intense and committing mixed routes of Heinrich, Harmston, Wagner, and Colbert have focused considerable national and international attention on Maple.

A more extensive climbing history of the area will be available in Jason Stevens's *Maple Canyon Ice Climbing.* Stevens has done a superb job of organizing the routes and making sense of scattered and incomplete information. Early records had been sketchy or lost entirely, while many of the most recent high-end routes have not been repeated, and their locations are unclear. In spite of these stumbling blocks, Stevens's guide includes detailed information on over 80 distinct routes, with more to be added by the time it's available in the fall of 2000.

THE SAN PITCH MOUNTAINS

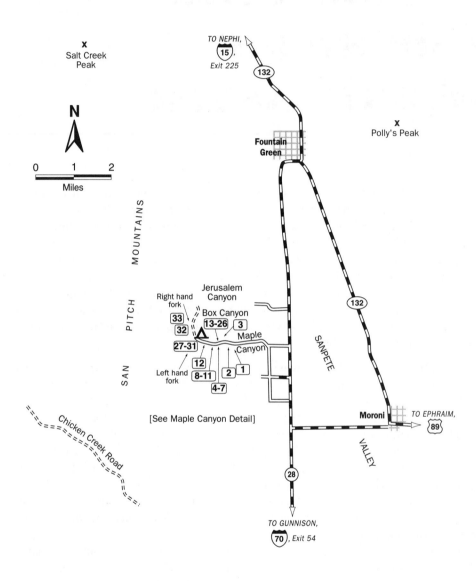

x
Salt Creek
Peak

N

0   1   2
Miles

TO NEPHI,
15,
Exit 225

132

x
Polly's Peak

Fountain Green

M O U N T A I N S

S A N   P I T C H

132

Jerusalem
Canyon

Right hand
fork

Box Canyon

33   **13-26**   **3**

32

Maple

27-31

Canyon

12

Left hand
fork

8-11   **2**   **1**

4-7

S A N P E T E

Chicken Creek Road

[See Maple Canyon Detail]

Moroni   TO EPHRAIM,
89

V A L L E Y

28

TO GUNNISON,
70, Exit 54

Getting there: From Interstate 15, take exit 225 at Nephi, then head east on Utah 132 through a canyon to the town of Fountain Green. Follow signs south to Maple Canyon. If approaching from I-70, exit at Salina and drive north on U.S. Highway 89. At a junction just north of Ephraim, turn left onto Utah 132. Follow it to Moroni, then follow the signs west to Maple Canyon. The dirt roads in the area are generally not plowed. At the mouth of the canyon there is a turnout large enough for several vehicles, and 0.1 mile farther up, at a diversion dam, is another pullout large enough for three or four vehicles. The canyon road is very narrow. DO NOT DRIVE UP THE CANYON UNLESS YOU HAVE 4-WHEEL DRIVE or the road is clear of snow. The hike or ski is negligible (15 minutes from the pullout to the first ice).

General Description: Maple Canyon has over 80 established routes with potential for many more. Lengths range from 20 to 200 feet. The climbing is at altitudes of from 6,200 to 7,200 feet on ice over conglomerate sandstone. IMPORTANT NOTE: 60m ropes are highly recommended, and are necessary for many ascents and descents in Box Canyon. The climbs are committing, and the ice is generally thin. Carry shorter screws, ice hooks, and extra webbing. Consider nuts (Stoppers), smaller cams, and a selection of thin-bladed and small angle pitons. Pins often work well at the edges of cobbles. Many routes have bolt-and-chain rappel stations. Helmets are highly recommended.

Finding the routes may be difficult for first-time visitors unless they're with another climber who knows the area. Readers are encouraged to compare Stevens's and Wagner's maps with the maps included here. Each is different. It is recommended that newcomers spend a few hours getting oriented.

In the Main Canyon, orient from the mouth of Box Canyon/Route 4 (*Yellow Rapture*) and the bridge/Route 12 (*Suicidal Tendencies*). Inside Box Canyon, orient from *Cobble Cruncher* (Route 15) alcove and from the falls that separate lower and upper Box Canyon. In the Left Fork, orient from the group campground near the mouth of that fork. Use the photographs to help establish a few additional landmarks.

For the purposes of this book, distances between routes in the Main Canyon have been measured with a tape measure. In lower Box Canyon, distances are tape-measured from the junction of the Main and Box Canyon streambeds.

Climbing season: January to early February is probably the best time for ice in Maple. Most of the routes result from the refreezing of melted snow. No snow, no ice.

Ethics and access: Box Canyon is private property. The author is aware of no efforts by the owner to exclude climbers from the canyon. Climbers should protect the opportunity to use the canyon by being courteous, not defecating or urinating in the canyon, limiting noise, and packing all garbage out.

Maps: USGS Fountain Green South.

Other guidebooks: *Maple Canyon Ice Climbing* by Jason Stevens (fall 2000).

Gear and guides: See Appendix B. Maple Leaf in Ephraim is Jason Stevens's establishment. It carries a selection of gear, and it's a good place to get updates on conditions.

Camping and accommodations: Maple Canyon campground is a fee area during the summer, but it's free in the winter. Ephraim and Nephi both have good hotels, and there are bed and breakfast establishments throughout the valley.

Services: Gas and groceries are available in most of the towns in the Sanpete Valley. Ephraim and Nephi are the closest towns with a good variety of shopping, food, and bank (cash) options.

Emergency services: Call 911 for all emergencies. Hospitals are located in Nephi, Gunnison, and Mount Pleasant. Cell phones will work down below the mouth of the canyon. Local resources for search and rescue and technical rescue are probably adequate for most scenarios. Specialty teams and air evac are available from the Wasatch Front. The Wasatch and Manti-LaSal avalanche forecast centers pay no particular attention to the San Pitch Mountains, but their advisories should provide a good general idea of the conditions in central Utah. See Appendix C for telephone numbers and websites.

Nearby climbing and skiing: Some ice has been done in Jerusalem Canyon, the next canyon north of Maple. There's good ice in Huntington Canyon and Joes Valley to the east, North Creek Canyon and Santaquin Canyon to the north, and Thistle Junction/Spanish Fork Canyon to the northeast. The Wasatch Plateau has excellent backcountry skiing with easy access from Fairview Canyon (Utah 31). The closest commercial skiing is Sundance in Provo Canyon.

MAIN CANYON

1. RUBBER CUP NAUSEA (WI3, I)

Length: 100 feet.

Approach: This is located about 0.65 mile above the car pullout at the mouth of the canyon. Time: 15–20 minutes. Find it on the south side, about 75 feet above the road, directly across from two large clefts on the north-side cliffs and 750 feet east of Box Canyon.

The Climb: Thirty feet of steep ice lead into a couloir.

Descent: Rappel from two bolts on a ledge to the left of the top of the route.

MAIN CANYON AND BOX CANYON DETAIL MAP

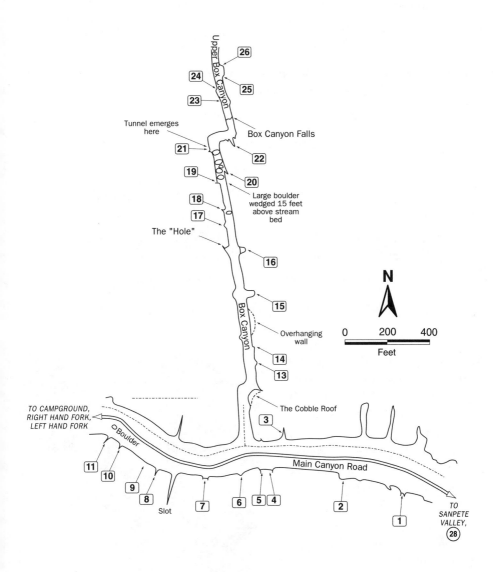

2. BOTTOMLESS TOPLESS (WI6 OR MI6, I)

Length: 180 feet.

Approach: This climb is located 292 feet west of Route 1, and 365 feet east of Route 4. Look for it in a large, left-facing corner on the south side, just above the road.

The Climb: Ascend a crack/corner (pins, small nuts, and cams), and trend left to the ice. The start and finish are usually thin.

Descent: Two-rope rappel from chain anchors on the dihedral to the right.

3. MORONI TURKEY PLANT A.K.A. MTP (WI3–4, I) ★

Length: 160 feet.

Approach: This route is in a deep, narrow cleft about 0.75 mile from the pullout, on the north side just above the road, 175 feet east of the mouth of Box Canyon.

The Climb: Climb a 25-foot pillar on the right wall of the cleft onto another 25-foot pillar on the opposite wall. Ascend thin, slabby ice for a pitch.

Descent: Rappel from two bolts under a roof on the left.

4. YELLOW RAPTURE (WI3, I) ★

Length: 90 feet.

Approach: This route is across the road and 100 feet east of the mouth of Box Canyon. Look for a laid-back face between 2 dihedrals.

The Climb: Ascend the ice to the right of the dihedral on the left side of the face. Often very thin at the bottom, with much thicker ice near the finish.

Descent: Rappel from a tree, or look for a bolt anchor to the left of the top of the route.

Mel Brown rappelling Yellow Rapture. Skidders *is to the right.*
BRIAN CABE PHOTO

5. SKIDDERS (WI3, I)

Length: 80 feet.

Approach: *Skidders* is on the same wall as Route 4, about 42 feet west of that route, just left of a shallow dihedral.

The Climb: Ascend this line to the right of the distinctive, overhanging boulder.

Descent: Rappel from bolts on the boulder or from a tree on the left.

6. RUNNING MAN (WI4, I)

Length: 180 feet.

Approach: This route is 108 feet west of Route 5, on the south side, just above the road.

The Climb: The route ascends a slab to a short, vertical bulge, through a couloir, and over another bulge.

Descent: Two-rope rappel from bolts to the right of the route.

Mel Brown on Running Man. BRIAN CABE PHOTO

7. TITANIC (WI6 OR M6, I) ★

Length: 165 feet.

Approach: Continue up the road 171 feet from Route 6. It's located on the south side, 160 feet to the east (left) of a small slot canyon.

The Climb: Climb a 50-foot slab onto a curtain and through a notch. Watch for 3 bolts to the left of the route.

Descent: Rappel from bolts to the right of the top of the route.

8. THE HOOKER (WI5, I)

Length: 180 feet.

Approach: This route is located in the back of a deep chimney on the south side, 85 feet west of the small slot, and 265 feet west of Route 7.

The Climb: Ascend a pillar to a curtain.

Descent: Rappel from a tree.

9. HOG JOWLS (WI3, I)

Length: 60 feet.

Approach: This is on the face about 58 feet to the west (right) of Route 5.

The Climb: A 60-foot smear.

Descent: Look for two bolts about 20 feet from the top of the route, above a small cave.

10. CHICKEN LIMBO (WI3, I)

Length: 80 feet.

Approach: Walk 156 feet west up the road from Route 9. *Chicken Limbo* is located on the wall on the south side, about 50 feet above the road and 67 feet east (left) of an obvious deep dihedral/chimney (Route 11).

The Climb: Climb thin slab ice to a tree.

Descent: Rappel from 2 bolts to the right of the route.

11. UNDER WRAPS (WI4, I) ★

Length: 100 feet.

Approach: This route lies in the back of the deep dihedral/chimney, 67 feet west of Route 10.

The Climb: Because of the proximity of the two opposing walls, this is a claustrophobic climb requiring a combination of delicate ice moves and stemming or chimneying.

Descent: Two-rope rappel from bolts on the right.

12. SUICIDAL TENDENCIES, A.K.A. SUICIDAL FAILURE (WI4, I)

Length: 180 feet.

Approach: About 1.25 miles from the pullout at the mouth of the main canyon is a south-side wall that comes down to within a few feet of a bridge. The route is in the center of this wall.

The Climb: Climb directly up the thin flow. Protection is marginal.

Descent: It's possible to rappel from slings around a giant cobble, which can be reached

Suicidal Tendencies, a.k.a. Suicidal Failure. BRIAN CABE PHOTO

via a snow/ice ramp up left above the top of the climb. Rappel into the next gully (east) of the climb. An alternative descent requires exposed scrambling up far enough to traverse west into a deep gully that drops to the road.

BOX CANYON (SEE MAP P. 135)

Box Canyon ("The Corridor") is the obvious slot canyon located on the north side of the road, 0.8 mile from the pullout at the mouth of the main canyon. The 200-foot vertical walls and steep gullies contain the best climbing in Maple Canyon. Box Canyon ice routes are not for the inexperienced climber. Most of the ice is thin and committing, and of the 30 or so established routes in the Box, only eight are in the WI2–4 range.

IMPORTANT DESCENT INFORMATION: Two ropes of 60m (200 feet) each are necessary for descents from most Box Canyon climbs. Climbers **CANNOT** rely on their 50m ropes to get them safely down. There are no midway rappel stations.

13. THE DAGGER (WI5–6 A1, I) ★★

Length: 150 feet.

Approach: This is located on the east wall, 445 feet from the stream junction at the mouth of Box Canyon.

The Climb: Climb about 30 feet to an arching roof. Aid the roof via 6 bolts to a curtain hanging from a shallow notch. Continue up the steep gully above. A bolt protects the exit moves.

Descent: Rappel from bolts.

14. TIED-OFF STUBBIES (WI5–6, I) ★

Length: 150 feet.

Approach: This is located 130 feet upstream from Route 13, at the right edge of an overhanging wall.

The Climb: A dangerous route. Climb the smear to the right of a shallow dihedral. The crux is at the top.

Descent: Rappel from a tree, or use the bolts on Route 13.

15. COBBLE CRUNCHER (WI4–5, I) ★★

Length: 110 feet.

Approach: This is the obvious, west-facing alcove and couloir in the east wall. It's located just over 800 feet from the mouth of Box Canyon, 245 feet upstream from Route 14.

The Climb: Ascend 70 feet of steep ice to a 35-foot vertical section. This route was the earliest of the steep routes in Box Canyon (first ascent: Valdez, 1982). It is one of the most reliable to form and generally has good ice.

Descent: Rappel from bolts.

16. SANDBAGGER (WI3–4 OR M4 I) ★

Length: 110 feet.

Approach: From Route 15, hike upstream 230 feet to a very obvious deep notch on the east wall.

The Climb: Follow the steep notch up to a ramp and the 40-foot crux (marginal ice or mixed). Natural pro. Carry some stoppers.

Descent: Rappel from a small tree.

Chris Harmston on Cobble Cruncher.
CHRIS HARMSTON COLLECTION

17. EMPIRE OF DIRT (WI5–6 OR M6, I)

Length: 200 feet.

Approach: From Route 16, walk upstream 120 feet to a notch on the west wall.

The Climb: Climb slabby ice to a roof. Ascend a hanging dagger into an alcove. Natural pro.

Descent: Rappel on two 60m ropes from a tree.

18. FROZEN LIZARDS (WI5–6, I) ★

Length: 200 feet.

Approach: This is located on the west wall, 85 feet upstream from Route 17.

The Climb: Climb a slab, trending right to a platform behind a gigantic flake. A curtain (crux) leads up and left. This can be done as a single long pitch with a 60m rope, or in two pitches, using the platform as a belay station.

Descent: Rappel from two bolts.

19. MAPLE MOON (WI5, I) ★★

Approach: Look on the west wall, 135 feet upstream from Route 18 and 20 feet downstream from a huge boulder wedged 15 feet above the streambed.

The Climb: Thin, steep ice on a slightly concave face to the right of a corner. Carry a selection of stoppers.

Descent: Rappel from two bolts. Care should be taken to not dislodge unstable ice just below the bolts. A small bush to the right and below these anchors has been used for rappels but is probably unsafe.

20. JESUS WEPT (WI6, I)

Length: 200 feet.

Approach: A thin arete is located behind some boulders 50 feet upstream from Route 19. This route is tucked in a north-facing chimney behind the arete.

The Climb: Climb slabs (very thin ice or mixed M6) to the left of the chimney/cave, then make a difficult, run-out, horizontal traverse right on verglass or rock to a vertical curtain. Use natural pro, pins, and nuts.

Descent: Rappel on two 60m ropes from two bolts.

Steve Mock leading Maple Moon.
BRIAN CABE PHOTO

21. MAPLE SYRUP (WI5–6, I) ★★

Length: 200 feet.

Approach: The route is found in a right-facing corner on the west wall, 155 feet upstream from Route 19, just above the spot where you emerge from the tunnel-like scramble beneath the final boulders that block the canyon.

The Climb: The name of this route refers to the odd color of the ice. Climb steep slab ice to 40 feet of difficult vertical-to-overhanging ice to chains. Include nuts and a selection of small angle pitons on the rack.

Descent: Two-rope rappel from two bolts.

22. DOS GUSANOS, A.K.A. TWO WORMS (WI5, I)

Length: 200 feet.

Approach: From the group of boulders mentioned in the previous description, continue upstream. The canyon makes an obvious turn east, then turns north again. This route is located in a deep, north-facing chimney 210 feet upstream from Route 21, about 75 feet downstream from Box Canyon Falls.

The Climb: Climb through the chimney for 65 feet, then up and left.

Descent: Rappel from a tree.

Maple Moon *(19) left,* Maple Syrup *(20) right.*
BRIAN CABE PHOTO

Doug Heinrich on Maple Syrup. CHRIS HARMSTON PHOTO

Note: Just upstream from Route 22, a falls blocks the canyon. This climb is called *Box Canyon Falls* (WI2, 45 feet). The area above the falls is referred to as Upper Box Canyon.

23. GOLDEN PLUMB (WI5, I–II)

Length: 150 feet.

Approach: This is located on the west wall, in a narrowed section about 100 feet upstream from the falls.

The Climb: Climb directly up a steep flow.

Descent: Rappel from two bolts.

24. GOLDEN SHOWER(S) (WI6 OR MI6, I–II) ★

Length: 160 feet.

Approach: From Route 23, hike about 60 feet up-canyon. This is on the west wall.

The Climb: Climb the slab (fixed pin) and surmount a curtain. Carry pins, cams, and nuts.

Descent: Rappel from a tree.

25. TEQUILA (WI3, I)

Length: 120 feet.

Approach: *Tequila* is found on a corner on the east wall, about 60 feet upstream from Route 24.

The Climb: Climb a steep smear to a tree.

Descent: Rappel from the tree.

26. PHEN-FEN (WI5 OR M6, I–II) ★★

Length: 120 feet.

Approach: This route can be found about 50 feet upstream from Route 25, on the east wall, in a right chimney/corner.

The Climb: This route ascends two columns and a steep, mixed gully. Watch for a couple of bolts for protection, and include a selection of stoppers on the rack.

Descent: Rappel from two bolts.

LEFT HAND FORK

The Left Hand Fork is reached in less than an hour (1.5 miles of hiking or skiing) from the pullout at the mouth of Maple Canyon's main canyon. This part of Maple Canyon has a good variety of shorter or easier routes.

27. BALD HEADED BABIES (WI5–6 OR M6, I)

Length: 100 feet.

Approach: 350 feet from the main canyon road. The route is located about 100 feet south of the petroglyph fence on the right side of a sport rock-climbing wall known as Engagement Alcove (see photo, page 147).

The Climb: Ascend a thin drip of ice protected with bolts.

Descent: Rappel from 2 bolts.

28. THE WET ITCHIES (WI4, I)

Length: 100 feet.

Approach: Hike a few yards south from Route 27. This route is located in the center of the alcove, right (north) of a shallow rib in the wall.

The Climb: Ascend the ice in a shallow depression. Without ice, this is a bolted 5.7 rock climb.

Descent: Rappel from bolt and chain sets.

29. BOWLING BALL HEAD (WI3–4, I)

Length: 100 feet.

Approach: This is south of Route 28 on the left side of the alcove.

The Climb: Ascend an obvious corner to a 2-bolt belay. Harder variations form to the right.

Descent: Rappel from trees above the climb.

30. SIR MIX-A-LOT (M6/WI6, I) ★

Length: 40 feet.

Approach: From Engagement Alcove walk 150 feet south, around a tower-like buttress on the right side of what climbers refer to as The Orangutan Wall.

The Climb: Ascend slabs past a bolt and continue up a difficult, right-side corner. Two bolts at the roof protect it to easier climbing above.

Descent: Rappel.

Engagement Alcove

Looking toward the Left Hand Fork *from the road near the campground. The upper reaches of* Engagement Alcove *are seen in the upper center of the photo.* DAVE BLACK PHOTO

Bowling Ball Head. CHRIS HARMSTON PHOTO

31. GET WHACKED (WI5–6, I)

Length: 130 feet.

Approach: This is on the left (south) side of The Orangutan Wall.

The Climb: This is the main flow left of the center of the wall.

Descent: Rappel from 3 bolts to the right.

RIGHT HAND FORK

A quarter-mile north of the campground is a small pullout. The right fork climbs are in the canyon to the left (west). Relatively little has been done, in spite of the enormous potential for new routes in this area.

32. FRANKENCHRIST (WI5–6, I)

Length: 150 feet.

Approach: Walk west 300 yards up the canyon from the pullout. The route is located on a crag to the left and can easily be seen from the road.

Kim Csizmazia on Frankenchrist. CHRIS HARMSTON PHOTO

The Climb: Climb chandeliered and curtained ice to the rim.

Descent: Rappel from bolts near a small tree.

33. ICE 800 (M8 OR WI5–6, I)

Length: 80 feet.

Approach: Hike west up the canyon from Route 32 about 0.8 mile, keeping to the left. This route is located about 100 yards down-canyon, near an enormous sport climbing cave rock climbers call *The Pipedream*. Time: 30 minutes. The climb is located above the feature known to rock climbers as the *Margarita Roof*, to the left of the cave.

The Climb: Follow what is essentially a bolt ladder (10 bolts).

Descent: Rappel.

THE WASATCH PLATEAU: JOES VALLEY

The 10,000-foot crest of the Wasatch Plateau catches the storms coming in from the west and pulls out the moisture like a sponge. The forested, red-walled mountains are a stark contrast to the San Rafael Swell to the east. Lying in the rain shadow of the plateau, the canyons of the Swell are carved out by a handful of streams and flash-flood washes that feed into the San Rafael River. The resulting range of environments and extremes gives us one of Utah's finest and least utilized recreational opportunities.

Author's Note: It's difficult for me to avoid writing in first person about this area. The two-and-a-half years (1991 to 1994) and three ice seasons I spent in residence in Orangeville and Joes Valley were a perfect recovery from seven bloody years as a paramedic in Ogden's knife-and-gun neighborhoods and northeastern Wyoming's cowboy frontier. I roamed the plateau solo and fell in love with it. Not once did I see another climber or even another climber's boot prints. It was my personal ice playground and I climbed nearly every day and many nights, blissfully unaware that Doug Coats and friends had explored most of these ice routes five years before.

In writing this book I had the privilege of meeting and sharing memories of Joes Valley with Doug Coats. For nearly two decades, Doug was one of Utah's most dedicated ice climbing explorers. It is interesting that after all these years and all our climbing in other places, it was Joes Valley that we both most wanted to return to.

Climbing history: Although some climbing in Joes Valley likely was in progress by the mid 1970s, the earliest recorded ice climbs in the Wasatch Plateau were Doug Coats's 1986 solo ascents of *CCC Falls*, the practice gullies, *Pterodactyl, Tyrannosaurus,* and *Brontosaurus (Bushdiver)*. In January and February of 1987, he returned with T. Thompson to climb *Wolfenstein (Melty Way)* and several other routes in both Joes Valley and Huntington Canyon. Conrad Anker, Mugs Stump, and Brian Smoot were also climbing in the area by then and had climbed most of *Spear of Fear*. Smoot, Stump, and Mark Galbraith climbed *Primadonna* in 1988. Also in 1988, Coats and Thompson climbed *Masterlock* and did the complete *Deadbolt*. In the 1991 to 1994 seasons, I soloed *Donorcicle, Spear of Fear,* the first routes at Mary's Lake, the complete *Amphitheater*, and the "Dog" routes at Slide Lake. In the late 1990s, many new routes were completed by Salt Lake City climbers, who by then were being attracted to Joes in droves. The most recent significant developments are Brian Cabe's routes at Mary's Lake, done in January and February of 2000.

Steve Mock leading Thunderbolt and Lightfoot *at Mary's Lake.* BRIAN CABE PHOTO

THE WASATCH PLATEAU

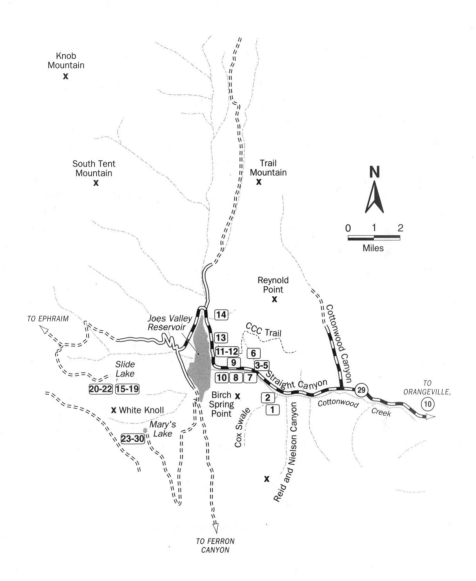

Getting there: From the Wasatch Front, take Interstate 15 south to Spanish Fork, then get on US 6 and take it to Price. From Price, take Utah 10 south to Huntington. South of Huntington, get on UT 29, which will take you to Orangeville and then Joes Valley Reservoir.

Climbers arriving from the east or west on I-70 should get off at exit 89 and take UT 10 north to UT 57 which leads to Orangeville. In Orangeville, get on UT 29 heading west to Joes Valley.

If coming from Fountain Green (Maple Canyon), drive east to Fairview, then get on UT 31 and take it east and southeast through Huntington Canyon.

Note: Watch for deer and elk on all these roads.

General Description: The routes described in this section range from 70 feet to a half-mile in length. They form over sandstone at altitudes of 5,500 to 9,600 feet. Most of the routes climbed to date are fat, and a good rack of ice screws will protect them.

Snow depths are generally minimal in Straight Canyon and around the lakeside routes. Approaches are easier, and there are fewer avalanche problems than in the Wasatch. Even so, always get an avalanche forecast. Helmets are recommended.

Climbing season: Joes Valley has both the earliest and longest season of any major ice climbing area in the state. By mid-November, many of the Straight Canyon and lakeside routes are in fat shape. The ice above Slide Lake can form in October and stay into April.

Ethics and access: All of the routes described here were ascended and descended without bolts. Still, bolts are starting to appear on many of these climbs despite an abundance of live timber, solid deadfall, boulders and cracks easily accessible for both rappelling and belaying. More conservative bolting practices are recommended.

Access has not been an issue. Nearly all of these routes are located in national forest. Some of the Huntington Canyon routes are on mining company lands. As long as climbers' vehicles aren't blocking truck access to the mines and loading areas, there probably won't be anything said. It's a good idea to notify the mine office when you're in the area.

Maps: Ferron Canyon (Mary's Lake); Joes Valley Reservoir; Mahogany Point; Rilda Canyon (Huntington Canyon); Hiawatha.

Other guidebooks: To date there's no comprehensive guide to either the rock or ice climbs of this area.

Gear and guides: Come with everything you think you'll need and more. The closest selection of gear is found at Maple Leaf in Ephraim. Provo is the nearest alternative. Check at those shops regarding guide services. Joes Valley is off the beaten path, but undoubtedly there's considerable "pirate" guiding going on there.

Camping and accommodations: There's a motel in Castle Dale and one in Huntington. Price has a better selection, plus it has a night life of sorts. Car campers in Huntington

Mugs Stump on the crux pillar of Spear of Fear. BRIAN SMOOT PHOTO

and Straight Canyons and in the pulloffs around the lake will be cold but are rarely hassled. The Joes Valley campgound on the west side of the lake keeps one area open in winter and does not charge a winter fee. Avoid car camping near the small communities on the north and southwest sides of the lake. The alcove at the base of *CCC Falls* is a pleasantly secluded bivy spot large enough for six or more. If you use it, please relieve yourself out of the drainage.

Services: Gas and groceries are available in Castle Dale and Huntington. Price has a wider selection of services.

Emergency services: Call 911 for emergencies. The nearest hospital is located in Price.

Nearby climbing and skiing: There are some amazing boulders in Straight Canyon and Cottonwood Canyon (Trail Mountain Mine road). Late in the season, it's not unreasonable to spend mornings on the ice and afternoons on the boulders. Down in the Swell there are plenty of cracks and small towers. The roads there can be nasty in poor weather. Good ice climbing is found in Maple Canyon to the west and in Price and Indian Canyons to the northeast.

STRAIGHT CANYON AND JOES VALLEY

A lot of ice routes have been done in Straight Canyon. Virtually every one of the south-slope gullies has ice. Only the longer or more interesting routes are described here.

Some very short routes have been done near the Wilberg Mine (on UT 57 north of UT 29); however, there may be access issues with the mining company. A few miles up UT 10 out of Orangeville is the Cottonwood Canyon Road. It cuts up north to the Trail Mountain Mine. There have been numerous flows seen in Cottonwood Canyon and several side canyons that feed into it from

Tim Thompson exiting the cave near the bottom of Cox Swale. DOUG COATS PHOTO

the east. A couple of 1- to 2-pitch low-angle gullies with short icicles and bulges have been climbed along the east side of the road about 0.25 mile down from the national forest boundary sign.

An ice "trail" with very short bulges and interesting boulders can be found at the mouth of Reid and Nielson Canyon at MM 7.9.

1. MASTERLOCK (WI2, II)

Length: Up to 1,500 feet or more.

Approach: Park at pullout MM 7.4 and cross the stream. This puts the climber in the mouth of what's known as Cox Swale ("swale" being another word for side canyon). Follow approach information for Route 2 to just under the headwall (60-foot curtain). *Masterlock* is the thornbush-choked gully left of the headwall.

The Climb: This is a long, low-angle thrash that ends twice without warning only to reappear in the next shallow gully to the right (west). When everyone in the party has had their fill of this masochistic endeavor, a long traverse right (west) will lead to Cox Swale and Route 2.

Descent: Hike and downclimb Route 2, as described below.

2. DEADBOLT, A.K.A. THE HIGHWAY TO HEAVEN (WI4–5, II–III) ★

Length: Up to 3,000 feet.

Approach: Park at the pullout at MM 7.4. Cross the stream and step onto the ice.

The Climb: Follow the floor of Cox Swale over gentle steps, through an interesting cave (see photo), to the base of a headwall, which consists of a 60-foot curtain. This is the crux and can be WI5 early in the season. Climb it, or skirt it to the left. Above the curtain, continue over more flats and easy bulges, a 30-foot column,

Robert Lang on Deadbolt.
BRIAN CABE PHOTO

and seemingly endless flat-footing ice until it disappears into the strata high in the Swale. This entire route is often free of snow. Under those conditions the climber is on ice for well over half a mile—a wide "highway" of ice. This is an extremely casual and enjoyable solo or night climb.

Descent: Hike down the route. The cruxes can be rappelled from trees or skirted to the east.

3. PREMADONNA, A.K.A. PRIMADONNA (WI5, I) ★★

Length: 200 feet.

Approach: Park at a pullout on the south side of the road at MM 6.2. The small canyon to the north holds Routes 3–6. Grunt up the crest of the right (east) slope and along the base of the cliff. Time: 30–45 minutes.

The Climb: Climb a long, steep but stepped curtain. The second pitch ascends the upper column into an alcove, then ascends the corner directly above, or traverses up through ledges on the right.

Descent: Rappel from trees.

4. UNNAMED (WI4–5, I)

Length: 200 feet.

Approach: From Route 3, continue traversing north along the base of the cliff band for about 75 feet.

The Climb: Steps and curtains to the rim.

Descent: Rappel from trees.

5. SLIP-SLIDIN' AWAY, A.K.A. SURPRISE PARTY (WI4–5, I)

Length: 200 feet.

Approach: From the base of Route 3, traverse 275 feet left (north).

The Climb: This route consists of several major steps to the canyon rim. There are often multiple lines available, but the formation can be very wet and thin.

Descent: Rappel from trees.

6. SPEAR OF FEAR (WI5–6, I–II) ★

Length: 200 feet.

Approach: From the pullout at MM 6.2, follow the streambed north for 0.5 mile, surmounting or skirting a few ice boulder moves.

The Climb: Climb two curtains, 45 and 60 feet. The second pitch ascends a cauli-

The Spear of Fear. DOUG COATS PHOTO

flower cone and a 60-foot dagger column. This is a superb climb in a remote and exposed setting.

Descent: Rappel from large trees.

7. BUSHDIVER, A.K.A. SMAUG (WI3–4, II)

Length: 800–900 feet.

Approach: Cross the stream at MM 6. If the stream is high it's possible to cross on a giant log a few hundred feet upstream from the climb (MM 5.9). The route starts at the bottom of the gully.

The Climb: Climb steppy ice for a long pitch to a 25-foot curtain. Easy steps and bulges and bushwhacking for about 600 feet lead to a stacked pair of 30-foot steps. The ice ends in the strata 100 feet above.

Descent: Scramble and downclimb. There are plenty of trees for rappels if needed.

8. TYRANNOSAURUS (WI2–3, I)

Length: 600 feet or more.

Approach: Cross the stream at MM 5.7 and enter the gully.

The Climb: This ascends a wide flow over a series of bulges. Early in the season, about halfway there are two 30-foot columns. Later in the season, these widen, connect, and become very easy to climb. Above them, follow easy ice until it fades.

Descent: Hike and scramble down the route. The bulges can be rappelled from trees or skirted to the east.

Note: At MM 5.5, between the road and the stream, are several flows originating from drainage pipes. These range up to 200 feet, with an interesting finish on the pipes.

9. THE AMPHITHEATER (WI6, I–II)

Length: 200 feet.

Approach: This route is on the north side, directly above a pullout at MM 5.4.

The Climb: Climb a 50-foot icicle curtain (or shorter curtains to the right), then work over two steps of 12 and 20 feet onto a large ledge-alcove. The second pitch ascends two 30-foot curtains and ends at the cone below the hanging 60-foot crux icicle (pitch 3).

Descent: Rappel from trees.

Mugs Stump on the first pitch of The Amphitheater. BRIAN SMOOT PHOTO

10. PTERODACTYL (WI3, I)

Length: 200–400 feet.

Approach: From the bottom of Route 8, traverse west to the base of the climb. This route is in the next major gully and is hidden by trees (MM 5.3).

The Climb: 100 feet of moderate ice to 2 steep, 20-foot steps. Continue until the ice fades.

Descent: Downclimb and scramble. Many trees.

Note: Between MM 4.6 and 6.0 along the north side are many steep 40- to 60-foot seeps that freeze and thaw with some regularity. They can be fun, but descents can be problematic. At MM 4.6, between the road and the lake is a huge pipe that creates an interesting 1–2 pitch stairway of ice with a 15-foot crux to the pipe.

11. WOLFENSTEIN, A.K.A. MELTY WAY (WI4–5, I) ★

Length: 200 feet.

Approach: This route starts at the road at MM 4.35.

The Climb: Ascend ice and scree to a 12-foot wall. Climb it to a large ledge. Ascend a 35-foot vertical section to another ledge, then another 12-foot wall to a belay. The second pitch follows moderately easy ice for 100 feet to a 30-foot stepped wall.

Descent: Rappel from trees.

Wolfenstein, a.k.a. Melty Way.
BRIAN CABE PHOTO

12. UNNAMED (WI5, I)

Length: 150 feet.

Approach: This starts a few yards above the road at MM 4.3, at the base of a large right-facing dihedral.

The Climb: Slightly stepped, but otherwise continuously vertical to the rim.

Descent: Rappel from trees.

13. CCC FALLS (WI4, I)

Length: 450 feet (including stream bed to crux).

Approach: *CCC Falls* lies in a canyon above MM 3.6. Park at a pullout at MM 3.7 and walk north. The easiest approach is along the crest of the north slope, where the snow is more shallow. It's also possible to hike directly up the streambed, through brush, and over a few small ice bulges.

The unnamed route (Route 12) just north of Wolfenstein. BRIAN CABE PHOTO

The Climb: Climb a steep 30- to 40-foot bulge, then follow the ice upward over smaller bulges for 70 feet. Watch for a set of bolts in a corner to the left, just below the rim. Just over the rim, follow the streambed over snow or low-angle ice for about 300 feet to a 25- to 30-foot vertical curtain.

Descent: From below the rim, rappel from the bolts. Those who continue above the rim can traverse right (south) to connect with the CCC Trail.

14. DONORCICLE (WI5, I) ★

Length: 140 feet.

Approach: At MM 2.8, drive, hike, or ski the dirt road east to the mouth of a small canyon. The route is hidden by large trees.

Donorcicle. BRIAN CABE PHOTO

The Climb: The climb is a single drop from the rim to the base. There is often a large cone.

Descent: Rappel from trees on the right or hike up the streambed until it's possible to traverse slopes to the south.

SLIDE LAKE

This is an area erroneously referred to as Josephite Point. It consists of two steep, 1,000-foot, north-facing walls denuded of vegetation and convoluted with ice-filled gullies. They sit high on the south slope of the Seely Creek drainage and can be reached only by snowmobile or skis from UT 29 (which turns into a miserable, narrow, dirt road west of Joes Valley Reservoir) then along the road to Pete's Hole Reservoir and Slide Lake. It could probably also be reached from above along Wagon Road Ridge. This is not an easy approach, and climbing parties should plan on spending the night. The left (east) face is the Wall of Good and the right (west) face is the Wall of Evil. It's possible to ski or snowmobile to within about 200 yards of these faces. Generally the gullies are low- to moderately-angled, with some long, steep bulges. Much of the ice is covered with snow. When not covered, they are incredibly long ice climbs. Be aware that these routes were initially soloed unroped and the distances given are conservative guesses by the first ascent party. The "Dog" routes are named for the first ascensionist's German shepherd, who chewed his snowmobile seat to shreds during a trip to Mary's Lake.

15. SCREW THE DOG (WI3, III)

Length: 700 feet.

Approach: By snowmobile or skis, as described above. The route is located on the eastern third of the Wall of Good, in a wide gully to the left of a crown of trees.

The Climb: Ascend snow and low-angle ice to a steep bulge midway before the gully

The Wall of Good. DAVE BLACK PHOTO

widens. The first ascent stayed along the right margin. The left side is probably easier. The ice tends to be thin or absent at the bottom of this gully.

Descent: It's a long hike around to the west to steep, timbered slopes and gullies. An option to consider on all of these routes is carrying some cut pipe or trash screws and extra webbing to leave behind for rappelling the routes. Double 60m ropes would speed the process along.

16. KILL THE DOG (WI3–4, III)

Length: 800 feet.

Approach: See page 164, Slide Lake.

The Climb: This is a wide gully of thick ice that ascends the wall to the right of the crown of trees. Climb snow and low-angle, then moderate ice. It steepens midway then lies back again for a pitch to another large bulge. The upper half of the route opens into a huge fan, and there are many variations possible. The first ascent party stayed to the left, climbing another several hundred feet over generally easy ice with some bulges.

Descent: See route 15.

17. SAN PEDRO JOURNEY (WI3–4, III)

Length: 900 feet.

Approach: See page 164, Slide Lake.

The Climb: Ascend snow and low-angle ice to a steep, midroute "step" into a couloir. As it widens out again, stay right toward the top.

Descent: See Route 15.

18. THE INCREDIBLE HULK (WI3, III)

Length: 1,000 feet.

Approach: See page 164, Slide Lake.

The Climb: *The Incredible Hulk* goes directly up the widest and deepest cleft in the Wall of Good. Climb low-angle ice or snow up to a thick flow of ice that progressively widens. Work over several steps. At the top of the steeper midroute pitches, the ice widens out in a huge fan. The first ascent party followed the left side several hundred feet to the tree line.

Descent: See Route 15.

19. SKIN THE DOG (WI3, II–III)

Length: 600–700 feet.

Approach: See page 164, Slide Lake.

The Climb: *Skin the Dog* is the gully to the right of Route 18. It almost merges with that route at the bottom. Climb this gully directly into trees low on the right side of the face.

Descent: See Route 15.

20. FLUSH AGAIN (WI4, III)

Length: 900 feet.

Approach: See page 164, Slide Lake.

The Climb: A low-angle gully to a very steep step. Finish into the trees.

Descent: See Route 15.

21. THE SPIRAL SHIT SMEAR (WI4, III)

Length: 1,000+ feet.

Approach: See page 164, Slide Lake.

The Wall of Evil. Dave Black photo

The Climb: This is a long, low-angle gully on the Wall of Evil, to the left of Route 22. The crux is the right (western) of two steep flows that can be seen draping over the cliff band near the top of the left side of the wall. Follow the gully up past some midway bulges and over the cliff band to the trees.

Descent: Hike east to timbered slopes leading down to the base of the wall.

22. NORTHERN LITE (WI2, III)

Length: 1,200–2,000 feet.

Approach: See page 164, Slide Lake.

The Climb: This is a long, low-angle gully that splits The Wall of Evil. It's usually packed with snow. Thrash up through the snow and over a few long ice bulges. The gully continues through the trees, and in a snow-free early season, a climber could probably stay on the ice for hundreds more feet.

Descent: Descend the gully or hike east to timbered slopes to the base.

MARY'S LAKE

Mary's Lake can be reached via the North Dragon Road (also known as the North Horn Mountain Road, although signs indicating either name may not be present), which runs along the west shore of the Joes Valley Reservoir and then south toward

Looking north along the cliffs above Mary's Lake. Route 26 is on the left. Route 29 is the large flow on the right. BRIAN CABE PHOTO

Ferron Canyon. Just past the south end of the reservoir, a dirt road forks right and west. Follow this road about 4 miles to Mary's Lake. Above the lake is a band of gray cliffs that are much steeper and farther away than they appear (30–60 minutes from the lake). The approach is usually through deep snow over steep talus and scree. It's believed that Brian Cabe's routes, done in January and February of 2000 with partners Steve Mock and Dwight Curry, are the first in the area since 1993. With the exception of the name for Route 28, the following information comes directly from Cabe's notes. All routes are somewhat steppy in nature and ascend straightforward lines from the base to the rim.

23. RABBIT STEW (WI3, I)

Length: 60 feet.

Approach: The cliff band above Mary's Lake directly faces the lake in cirque-like fashion: In other words, take the fall-line toward your route of choice.

The Climb: All Mary's Lake routes listed here are well defined, one-pitch routes. They average only 125 feet in length and can be generically described as a straight shot from base to rim, adequately protected with screws.

Descent: Rappel from a small tree.

MARY'S LAKE ROUTES

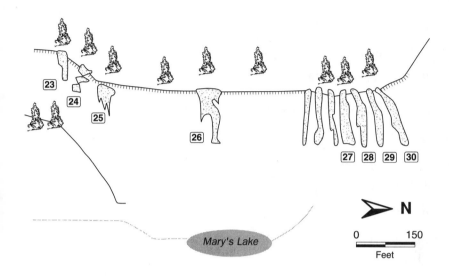

Mary's Lake

N

0   150
Feet

24. STEPPY (WI3–4, I)

Length: 80–100 feet.

Approach: See Route 23.

The Climb: See Route 23.

Descent: Rappel from trees.

25. WHITE SPIDER (WI4, I)

Length: 80–100 feet.

Approach: See Route 23.

The Climb: See Route 23.

Descent: Rappel from trees.

26. THUNDERBOLT AND LIGHTFOOT (WI5, I)

Length: 140 feet.

Approach: See Route 23.

The Climb: See Route 23.

Descent: Rappel from a large tree.

27. COOL WHITE STARE (WI4, I)

Length: 160 feet.

Approach: See Route 23.

The Climb: See Route 23.

Descent: Rappel from a small tree.

28. DIRTY BLONDE (WI4, I)

Length: 150 feet.

Approach: See Route 23.

The Climb: See Route 23.

Descent: Rappel from trees.

29. ALZCLEIMBERS (WI5, I)

Length: 140 feet.

Approach: See Route 23.

The Climb: See Route 23.

Descent: Rappel from trees.

30. ROUND THE CORNER (WI3–4, I)

Length: 150 feet.

Approach: See Route 23.

The Climb: See Route 23.

Descent: Rappel from trees.

The bench below the cliffs at Mary's Lake is known as the Water Terrace. It runs from Mary's Lake to Josephite Point, then around to the Slide Lake area. Ice similar to that at Mary's Lake has been spotted in some of the small canyons and cliffs above the terrace between Mary's Lake and the Wall of Good.

HUNTINGTON CANYON

The Huntington Canyon routes are all reached along UT 31 east of Huntington. There are flows in Deer Creek and the North Fork of Meetinghouse Canyon. The roads into these canyons are accessed between the power plant and Bear Creek Campground (MM 39).

At MM 38.3 is a Co-op Mine road into Bear Creek Canyon. As you drive up this canyon, note a long, seeping wall above the baseball diamond. Doug Coats has referred to this as the Wonder Wall. When conditions are right, a 400-foot wide wall of ice forms, with dozens of pillars, steps, and faces. Higher in the right fork of Bear Creek Canyon is a series of overhung crags that produce a column/cone formation very similar to but longer than the *Spear of Fear* in Joes Valley. To date it probably hasn't been climbed. The following route is located in the main (left) fork of the canyon.

31. SCHOOL GULLY (WI1–2, I)

Length: 600 feet.

Approach: Drive up the switchbacks on the road to the upper area of the Co-op Mine. Park at the base of the main (left) fork. There have not been access problems in the past, but park well out of the way of descending coal trucks. Hike and scramble directly up the canyon for about 0.67 mile. On the north slope is a low-angle gully just steep enough to keep the snow off. Climb directly up the gully, over a few bulges until it disappears into the scree slope.

Descent: Scramble down the steep scree to the left of the climb.

Note: A little more than 0.5 mile upstream from Route 31 is *Bear Creek Falls* (45-foot column).

Note: Back in Huntington Canyon, at MM 38, on the north side above the road is an ugly half-pitch seep that has been climbed (WI4–5) but is usually very thin and difficult to protect.

32. INSPIRED BY GRAVITY (WI4–5, I)

Length: 80 feet.

Approach: At MM 34.6 on the south side of the canyon is this nice little climb in a notch hidden by trees. Park at a pullout, cross the stream and bushwhack to the base of the climb (20 minutes).

The Climb: Ascend a 2-tiered, 60-foot column/curtain to easier ice.

Descent: Rappel from trees.

HUNTINGTON CANYON DETAIL

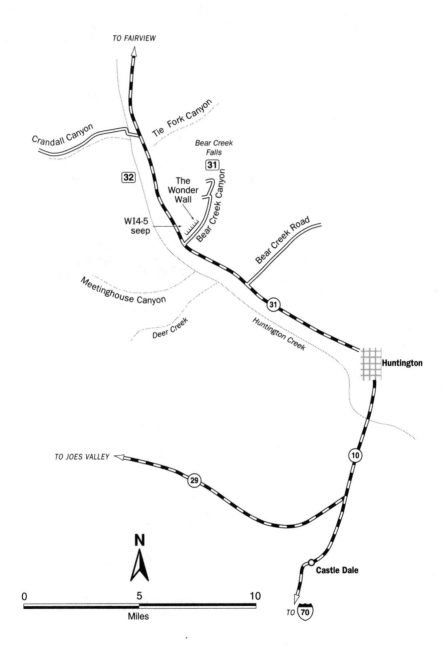

TO FAIRVIEW

Tie Fork Canyon

Crandall Canyon

Bear Creek Falls

[31]

[32]

The Wonder Wall

Bear Creek Canyon

WI4-5 seep

Bear Creek Road

Meetinghouse Canyon

(31)

Deer Creek

Huntington Creek

Huntington

TO JOES VALLEY

(29)

(10)

N

Castle Dale

TO (70)

0   5   10
Miles

Doug Coats on Inspired by Gravity. TIM THOMPSON PHOTO—DOUG COATS COLLECTION

The turnoff to Crandall Canyon is located at MM 33. Several climbs have been done in this canyon. Up this road 1.2 miles, just before the mine, is a deep, narrow canyon/gully to the east. The short ice curtains there have been climbed but are probably not worth the slog across the stream. This gully is a wind tunnel and avalanche collector. It's usually packed deep with snow, and mini-cornices form over the edges of the ice curtains. At MM 31.5 are some 50-foot seeps over cliffs on the north slope above the road.

SOUTHERN UTAH

This includes the area south of U.S. Highway 50 and Interstate 70. Here are Utah's finest geographic gems: a dozen national parks, monuments, and recreation areas. That's a lot of ground to cover in a single chapter, but the sad fact is that to date there has not been a lot of ice climbed. There is plenty of talk about gargantuan ice flows in Zion and in the redrock slots between there and Moab. It's not uncommon to see thick verglas coating large north-facing walls in Kolob Canyon. It's impossible to drive US 89, Utah 12, UT 14, and the road to Brian Head without noticing the daggers that are forming over undercut sandstone crags. This is a matter of being in the right place at the right time.

Getting there: The Tushar Mountains (Elk Meadows and Bullion Canyon) are bordered on the east by US 89 and on the west by I-15. To the south, Zion National Park and Cedar Canyon can be accessed from I-15 and US 89. I-70 joins I-15 just north of the Tushars and is the primary access highway to points east. US 191 south from Crescent Junction serves Moab redrock country and the La Sal Mountains.

General Description: This is such a large area that a general description is difficult. The climbs described in this chapter can be summarized, with notable exceptions, as short routes over sandstone at moderate altitudes.

Climbing season: Short. The exception is Cascade Falls in the Tushars. With its northern exposure and 9,000-foot altitude, it forms very early and stays late.

Ethics and access: In this part of Utah access is more a question of tenacity and patience than of property squabbles. Be courteous and observe property postings. Check at the national park visitor centers for regulations on backcountry permits and overnight excursions into the backcountry. Area closures for the protection of endangered species are not uncommon.

There is an enormous misconception about the need to bolt sandstone. There are many alternatives, and climbers should take the time to consider them. In the canyons of southern Utah, the clean purists will often chop bolts, leaving bolt addicts with no other choice than to slam in a few more bolts. If no bolts have been placed and there are alternatives to bolts, use them. If bolts have already been placed, preserve them.

Maps: USGS: Mt. Brigham (Bullion Canyon); Moab; Big Bend; The Windows Section; Kanab; Flanigan Ranch (Cedar Canyon); Brian Head; Parowan.

SOUTHERN UTAH

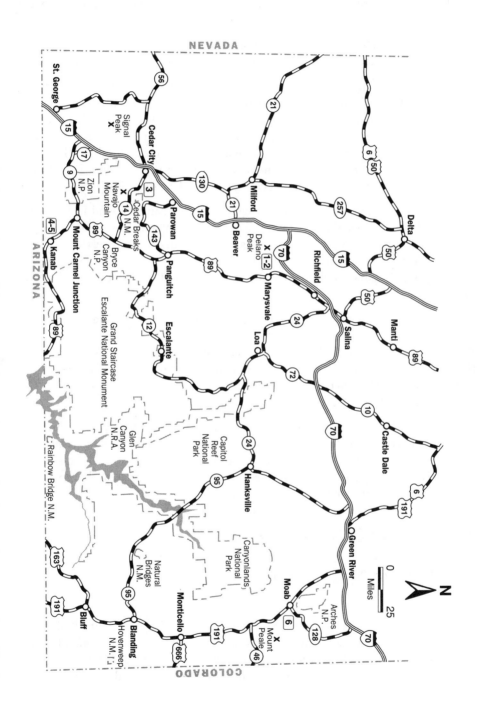

Other guidebooks: There are numerous guides to rock climbs, slot canyons, summits and hikes in southern Utah. Most climbing shops and large bookstores will have the best of them.

Gear and guides: There are climbing shops in St. George, Cedar City, and Moab. Ice climbing guides are likely to be as scarce as the ice. Check at the climbing shops.

Camping and accommodations: Southern Utah does a brisk summer tourist trade. There are motels and commercial campgrounds even in many of the small towns near the parks and along I-15. Off-season (winter) rates are often extremely reasonable. Car camping is definitely an option; southern Utah is warmer than northern Utah, and there are far fewer people to hassle with in the winter. Avoid St. George and Moab during spring break unless you want to share those cities and the wilderness around them with a mob of partying college and high school kids.

Services: An acceptable and reliable range of services can be found in St. George, Cedar City, Kanab, Richfield, Salina, Beaver, Panguitch, and Moab. Do not assume that a community that looks significant on your road map has the services you need. Many of those "towns" are little more than a gas station at a junction. Some services near the national parks shut down in the off-season, and plenty of others shut down on Sunday.

Emergency services: Call 911 for all emergencies. Cell phone coverage is not reliable throughout much of this region. Hospitals are located in St. George, Cedar City, Beaver, Kanab, Panguitch, Moab, Monticello, and Page. Air evac is available from the Wasatch Front, Las Vegas, Page, and Grand Junction. The mountains of southern Utah pick up their fair share of snow, and there have been avalanche fatalities. Get a forecast (Appendix C).

Nearby climbing and skiing: Elk Meadows and Brian Head are southern Utah's commercial ski destinations. The La Sal mountains near Moab are very popular with backcountry skiers. The sandstone climbing in this part of Utah is endless, and the altitude is low enough and temperatures warm enough in some areas that rock climbing is not unusual in winter.

TUSHAR MOUNTAINS

1. BULLION FALLS (WI4, I)

Length: 60 feet.

Approach: From Marysvale on US 89 drive west on Center Street into Bullion Canyon and continue until stopped by the snow. Ski or hike on the snowmobile-packed road past old mines and ghost towns until reaching a small bridge at what seems like the end of the canyon. From the bridge, a trail to the right (buried in deep snow) goes up to a marked viewpoint. Thrash to the base of the falls from there. Time: An hour or so (less by snow machine or ATV). This is an extremely enjoyable tour on skis.

The Climb: A 60-foot stepped column into the gully.

Descent: Rappel the route and return along the approach route or work down forested slopes to the east to the road.

2. CASCADE FALLS (WI3, I)

Length: 500 feet.

Approach: This is located several hundred feet south and uphill from the bridge, in the Cascade Creek drainage, which drops directly north into Bullion Canyon.

The Climb: A few big, moderately steep steps and notches up to 60 feet with some snow-slogging in between. The route is far more difficult in early, thin conditions (late October-November) than later in the season.

Descent: Descend via slopes to the left (southeast) of the route, or rappel the route.

Note: Across the stream, on the north slope, a low-angle, south-facing gully climb occasionally forms. Look for it a few hundred yards east of the bridge (WI1–2, several hundred feet in length).

PAROWAN AND CEDAR CANYONS

In Parowan Canyon on the way to Brian Head Ski Area, there are some very impressive rope-length spits of ice which occasionally form off the overhanging rims of the roadside crags known as The Beehives along the east side of UT 143 from MM 10.5 to 10.7. These are so close to the road and so obvious that it's hard to imagine they haven't been climbed. Lower in the canyon, *Hidden Haven Waterfall* offers some ice bouldering for those willing to suffer the approach into it.

In Cedar Canyon (UT 14) there are numerous seeps up to 50 feet in length between MM 6 and MM 10.

3. CEDARCICLE (WI5, I)

Length: 130 feet.

Approach: This is located across the stream at MM 9.9. Time: 5–10 minutes.

The Climb: Easy ice to a narrow, 80-foot vertical pillar.

Descent: Rappel from trees.

Other routes: At MM 10.1, across the stream is a 100-foot thin flow over steppy slabs. Just past MM 14 to the east is an enormous red-cliff bowl. Midway up this

Cedarcicle. BRIAN SMOOT PHOTO

bowl is an 80- to 100-foot pillar, and to its left are several smears and curtains of equal size. Probably an hour approach to get into them.

KANAB

Just north of town, immediately south off US 89 at MM 70.8 is a steppy, half-pitch WI2 flow.

4. MOQUI HOLDOUT (WI3–4, I)

Length: 80 feet.

Approach: Directly across from the commercial Moqui Cave tourist site at MM 70.5, hike 10 minutes up a small side canyon.

The Climb: A steep, 70–80-foot apron.

Descent: Rappel from trees.

5. MOQUI SLIDE (WI2–4, I)

Length: 70–80 feet.

Approach: At MM 70.2, just west of the Kanab Canyon Road turnoff, look south into a side canyon. It's a 15–20-minute hike across private property to the base of the climb.

The Climb: A fat, steep, half-pitch apron leads into a gully. If there's no snow, the climber can scramble over low-angle ice for another 1–2 pitches.

Descent: Rappel from trees.

MOAB AREA

Author's Note: In the local climbing shop, if you ask where the ice is, they'll probably tell you there isn't any. One warm February morning a few weeks before this manuscript went to the publisher, I went into the shop and asked (for the third time) where the ice was. The answer was the same: there isn't any, and everybody in Moab "just goes to Ouray." Within a couple of hours of that very conversation I spotted ice in several gullies along UT 128 and the Onion Creek Road and was able to climb one of these flows. They were easily visible from the road and undoubtedly had been climbed before. Don't believe everything you hear from the locals—there *is* ice near Moab.

Throughout the writing of this book I tried to respect the concerns of people who asked me to refrain from including material that would undermine important personal first-ascent projects or adversely affect an area in some way. In the case of the La Sal Mountains, several people expressed concern that including a small cluster of insignificant ice climbs there would have a negative effect on the local bear population if bunches of climbers showed up. Hence, those routes are not described here.

For those who simply must climb ice in the Moab area, there are some flows up Negro Bill Canyon and Onion Creek. There are many ice boulder problems and short routes in the gullies along UT 128 (check, for instance, at MM 2.5 and at MM 7.3 across from the Hal and Oak Grove recreation sites).

6. UNNAMED (WI3–4, I–II)

Length: Up to 450 feet.

The Climb: From Utah 128 at MM 11.8, hike east into a side canyon and scramble up the drainage for 30–45 minutes to the base of a 30-foot black face and corner. Climb the wet or mixed face, and above it ascend a chunky gully and minor bulges a rope-length to the base of a 25-foot cliff band. Climb thin ice, or dry-tool a break in the cliff on the right side. Ascend thin, low-angle ice over slickrock and thicker ice over bulges for a rope-length to another 25-foot cliff band. Climb either a dagger column in the middle of the overhanging cliff or curtains several yards to the left and right of the dagger. Continue on steppy ice up to yet another 25-foot overhung cliff band. Finish via the central curtain or in a fat corner to the right. It's possible to avoid the black face by hiking up a dirt ridge on the left (north) side of the canyon to a point where a traverse can be made to the base of the first cliff band.

Descent: Rappel from trees.

OTHER SOUTHERN UTAH AREAS

A number of columns and daggers have been done in remote slots in Zion. There are many rumors of long routes in Kolob Canyon and other parts of Zion.

Some very short and unreliable routes can be found in Kannaraville, Camp Creek, the Coral Pink Sand Dunes area, and Panguitch. Some years ago, a Warren Miller ski movie showed an aerial shot of a steep, 300-foot ice flow near Cedar Breaks. Highly transient flows of all sizes and angles can be seen at times from most of the state highways that traverse the mountainous terrain between Zion and Torrey. Lower Calf Creek Falls, a real prize located in the Grand Staircase–Escalante National Monument, has occasionally been seen in near climbable condition. Cascade Falls is a popular summer tourist hike near Navajo Mountain east of Cedar City. The falls are at high altitude, and the stream drops into the North Fork of the Virgin River and Zion Canyon. Parts of it certainly would be of interest to ice climbers.

APPENDIX A

GUIDEBOOKS

Desert Rock series by Eric Bjornstad (Falcon Publishing). This series of five rock climbing guides has replaced Bjornstad's original *Desert Rock* book.

Canyoneering: The San Rafael Swell, by Steve Allen (University of Utah Press, 1992).

Logan Canyon Climbs, by Tim Monsell.

Maple Canyon Ice Climbing, by Jason Stevens. Possibly available fall 2000. Contains over 80 routes and some excellent maps.

Maple Canyon Rock Climbing, by Jason Stevens, 1999.

Utah Ice, by Tim Wagner, 1999. This is a nice, small, inexpensive photocopy style guide available in a few shops. Hopefully Wagner will continue to revise it each season, as it will probably be the only way to keep up-to-date on mixed climbs.

Rock Climbing Utah, by Stewart Green (Falcon Publishing, 1998).

The Chuting Gallery, by Andrew McLean (Paw Prince Press, 1998).

Utah Mountaineering Guide, by Joe Kelsey, 1997.

GUIDE WEBSITES

The Intermountain Ice Project http://www.iceclimb.com/grade.html

The Utah Ice Climbing Guide http://www.kingsleymc.com/Clark/UtahIce.html

Rock & Ice Online Conditions http://www.rockandice.com

MAP SOFTWARE

3-D Topo Quads, Delorme 1999.

All Topo Maps: UTAH, iGage 1998.

APPENDIX B

CLIMBING SHOPS AND GUIDE SERVICES

Cedar City
Cedar Mountain Sports
921 South Main Street
Cedar City, Utah 84721
435-586-4949

Ephraim
Maple Leaf
480 South 50 East
Ephraim, Utah 84627
435-283-4400

Logan
Adventure Sports
51 South Main
Logan, Utah 84321
435-753-4044

The Trailhead
117 North Main
Logan, Utah 84321
435-753-1541

Moab
Moab Climbing Shop
550 North Main
Moab, Utah 84532
435-259-2725

Ogden
Black Diamond
3701 Washington Boulevard
Ogden, Utah 84403
385-399-9365

Canyon Sports
705 West Riverdale Road
Riverdale, Utah 84405
385-621-4662

Smith and Edwards
3936 North Highway 126
Ogden, Utah 84404
385-731-1120

Orem
(shop and guide service)
Hansen High Adventure
Specialities
757 North Main Street
Orem, Utah 84058
385-226-7498

Provo
Mountainworks
32 South Freedom Boulevard
Provo, Utah 84601
385-371-0223

Salt Lake City
Black Diamond
2084 East 3900 South
Holladay, Utah 84124
801-278-5552

International Mountain
  Equipment (IME)
3265 East 3300 South
Holladay, Utah 84109
801-484-8073

Kirkham's
3125 South State Street
South Salt Lake City, Utah
84115
801-486-4161

REI-Recreational Equipment
  Inc.
3285 East 3300 South
Holladay, Utah 84109
801-486-2100

Wasatch Touring
702 East 100 South
Salt Lake City, Utah 84111
801-359-9361

Exum Utah Mountain
Adventures (guide service)
2092 East 3900 South
Holladay, Utah 84124
801-550-EXUM
www.exum.ofutah.com

Canyon Sports
1844 East 7000 South
Holladay, Utah 84121
801-942-3100

APPENDIX C

EMERGENCY AND AVALANCHE/WEATHER/ICE FORECAST NUMBERS AND WEBSITES

Ambulance, Fire, Rescue, Sheriff, Police (all areas)	911
Avalanche and Weather Forecast	
Provo	385-378-4333
Salt Lake City	801-364-1581
Alta	801-742-0830
Park City	801-658-5512
Ogden	385-626-8700
Logan	435-797-4146
Moab	435-259-7669
Website	http://www.avalanche.org
Ice Conditions	http://www.rockandice.com

INDEX

ABOUT THE AUTHOR

Dave Black did his first ice climb on an obscure waterfall near Brigham City in 1967. Although he's done much of his living and climbing in other states and on other continents, he has returned to climb Utah's ice for 28 of the last 32 seasons. Black has explored Utah and the world as a climber, caver, canyoneer, and guide, and has logged many first ascents and descents. He's written several articles for American climbing magazines and many of his climbing and caving experiences have been profiled in outdoor journals and news media in North and South America and the Middle East.